G000161978

Opera

QUADRILLE

INTRODUCTION

'Why are they singing and why should I listen?' With opera, this is the perennial question. It's also one you have probably asked yourself at some point. Why tell a dramatic story not in speech but in song? I have certainly been asked it dozens of times; by ten-year-olds I was encouraging to dip their toes into opera for the first time; by nervous interns at the Royal Opera House and by investment bankers who usually spend their Saturday nights at clubs in London's East End, among many others.

There is nothing surprising about the question. For newcomers, traditional opera can often seem an odd activity. However, what did take my breath away was being asked that very same question when I worked at English National Opera (ENO) 20 years ago – not by a child or an intern or a potential sponsor but by the most gifted English composer of his generation. Mark-Anthony Turnage had already carried off the coveted first prize at a major German opera festival and had been commissioned to write a new work for ENO to be performed at the London Coliseum, the largest lyric theatre in Europe. Yet he was as sceptical about opera as the trainee researcher or the tyro banker. With one international success under his belt and another on the horizon, he was still wondering why characters chose to express their hopes and passions and fears not by speaking, but by singing.

The knowledge.
Opera | Dennis Marks

Publishing consultant Jane O'Shea
Editor Simon Davis
Creative director Helen Lewis
Art direction & design Claire Peters
Illustrator Claire Peters
Production Vincent Smith, Tom Moore

First published in 2015 by
Quadrille Publishing Limited
www.quadrille.co.uk

Quadrille is an imprint of Hardie Grant.
www.hardiegrant.com.au

Text © 2015 Dennis Marks
Design and layout © 2015
Quadrille Publishing Limited

Cataloguing in Publication Data:
a catalogue record for this book
is available from the British Library.

ISBN 978 184949 622 3

Printed in the UK

'Opera is an exotic and irrational entertainment, which has always been combated, and has always prevailed' remarked great English critic, poet and lexicographer Samuel Johnson. He found it irrational because they were singing rather than speaking and considered it exotic because he could not understand what they were singing about. Commentators still quote Johnson 300 years later, but they tend to remember the first half of the quotation and forget the rest. Yes, it is exotic and irrational and yes, it has always been combated (not least by those who have to pay for it). Yet, as Johnson ruefully admits, it has always *prevailed*, and it does so to this day.

Without question opera is loved and hated today with the same fervour that it was when it conquered England in the 18th Century, and every month you can read the popular press complaining about public money being spent on such a minority taste. Yet whether at the World Cup or on reality television, in arenas in Italy or in cinemas in the suburbs, opera has found its way into the hearts and minds of every generation and class. But what gives this strange activity the power to inspire the novice and obsess the enthusiast? What makes us suspend our disbelief and return to it again and again? Why, for all its absurdity, does opera seem to refresh the parts that other art forms cannot reach?

These are some of the questions this book hopes to tackle. If you're already part of the opera audience you may be able to guess at some of the answers, while if you find yourself approaching opera for the first time, you'll be pleased to find you have a few aids that were not available to the good Doctor Johnson in the 18th century. For most of the past 100 years, audiences have been able to hear traditional operas sung in their own language (in English at venues such as Glimmerglass in upstate New York, or my own previous home of the London Coliseum), while since the 1990s surtitles have offered simultaneous translation every bit as effective as subtitles in the movies.

The removal of the language barrier hasn't been the only development. Over the centuries, opera has also crept closer to our own familiar world – the irrational plots and stylized action largely replaced by something closer to the naturalistic drama of live theatre or cinema. In recent years, composers have even drawn their material from the front pages of the popular press or the latest television news bulletins. Turnage's most recent opera *Anna Nicole* re-tells the tabloid tale of a Playboy centerfold. The American composer John Adams forged a full-length work from Richard Nixon's diplomatic mission in China, while English composer Tansy Davies draws on the events of 9/11 in *Between Worlds* to create breathtakingly powerful drama. Surely it must now be possible to approach opera with the same open minds that we bring to straight theatre, film and television?

Yet many of us still cannot get over the central fact that the characters up on the stage sing rather than speak. But why should this be difficult to swallow? In a world that has lived with musical theatre since the days of Jerome Kern, this ought not to be a problem. Opera is no less realistic than *Showboat* or *Carousel*. Most of us have no problem with Maria crooning that the hills are alive with the sound of music or Sweeney Todd singing a love song to his naked razors. Indeed the sheer intensity of the experience is what persuades us to suspend our disbelief, and may well be the reason for Johnson's grudging admission of opera's enduring success. The magic, as it were, is in the music.

Music is and always has been a mind-altering substance. From ancient Greece to Madison Square Gardens, it has inspired ecstasy and hysteria for millennia. In *The Bacchae* of Euripides (which has more than once been set as an opera)

THE POWER OF MUSIC

The history of opera is packed with examples of music's mind-altering powers. In the early days of Italian opera, the gravity-defying top notes of celebrated castratos such as Senesino and Farinelli prompted respectable society ladies to fall into erotic trances. When Wagner's feverishly carnal *Tristan und Isolde* (*see* pages 84–5) was premiered two centuries later, some critics believed it should be banned because of the violent erotic reactions it provoked.

the followers of Dionysus are provoked to violent delirium by music. Operatic epiphanies needn't always be violent – from my own early experiences I can list a dozen moments when the fusion of words and music has stopped my heart. When the unfaithful Count in *The Marriage of Figaro* begs on his knees for forgiveness from his wife, the shape of the melody and the changes in the harmony that underpin it have crept under my skin. When Wotan bids farewell to his beloved daughter in *Die Walküre* and surrounds her with magic fire, the sound of the god's voice riding above Wagner's surging horns has brought a lump to my throat. And when Madama Butterfly (*see* pages 90–1) undertakes her long vigil – waiting for a husband who we know has abandoned her – the humming chorus of her fellow geishas has helped to sear the moment in my memory forever.

Characterization and staging make an essential contribution to the whole, but opera's standout scenes have the power to hit this same musical G-spot whether experienced in a 20,000 seater amphitheatre in Verona or through a pair of digital headphones.

If this is why they tell their stories in song rather than speech, what is the special sorcery that composers employ to make opera, of all the dramatic forms, so unforgettable? This is the trickiest of all questions – if it were not we would all be budding Verdis or Strausses. Nevertheless, it is one that this book will hope to shed some light on. While subjective and far from comprehensive, it may just, I hope, lead you to some life-changing operatic experiences of your own.

1 WHAT IS OPERA AND WHAT MAKES IT DIFFERENT?

Four centuries ago, music, theatre and dance came together in Italy to create the art form we now call opera. Over time the sound of its music has changed but the essence of opera has not: accompanied by an orchestra, with scenery, costumes and light adding drama, singers tell a story. But what is it that makes this story told through words and music different from regular drama?

STORY AND DRAMA IN OPERA

Born as music theatre, that is, music set to a libretto for the stage, opera has always valued a good story. And while there may be a number which stretch our credulity and patience, many of the finest are drawn from highly regarded literature – Mozart was drawn to the radical dramatist Beaumarchais for his libretti, Verdi constantly returned to Shakespeare, Puccini crafted libretti from successful contemporary fiction while Tchaikovsky chose to adapt the work of Russia's greatest poet Pushkin.

It is by comparing some of these literary and operatic works that we are able to demonstrate the mysterious effect that music can have on even the most familiar narrative. To take one example, Beaumarchais' controversial play *Le Nozze di Figaro (The Marriage of Figaro)* was already famous when Mozart and his librettist da Ponte made a bid to transform it into an opera.

The pair had to battle with the Austrian Emperor for permission to adapt such a provocative work, its notoriety growing largely from its revolutionary sentiments and plot – the story of an aristocrat defeated by his valet had great appeal for a mass audience shortly after the French revolution. But what could music add to this already successful satirical comedy?

In a word, humanity. And not simply in the tender and melancholy melodies Mozart gives to the betrayed Countess Almaviva, lovely though they are. Humanity is also found in music's unique ability to reflect complex human relationships by doing several things at once. At the end of the opera's third act, the farcical plot comes to a head with Figaro, preparing to marry the Countess' maid Susanna, unexpectedly trapped into a previously arranged marriage contract with the mature Marcellina... only for it to suddenly be revealed that he is actually Marcellina's long-lost illegitimate child. At this point there are six characters on stage, each with a different and conflicting aim – a complicated enough situation for a theatrical farce – yet when Mozart turns it into a musical sextet it soars to new comic levels. Its recurring melodies are taken up and transformed by each character; the same words ('your mother' and 'your father') sung to the same tune by six very different voices from lyric soprano to gruff bass as the reactions to Figaro's origins becoming increasingly comic, while the humour is intensified by a particularly sweet tune that changes key with each new revelation.

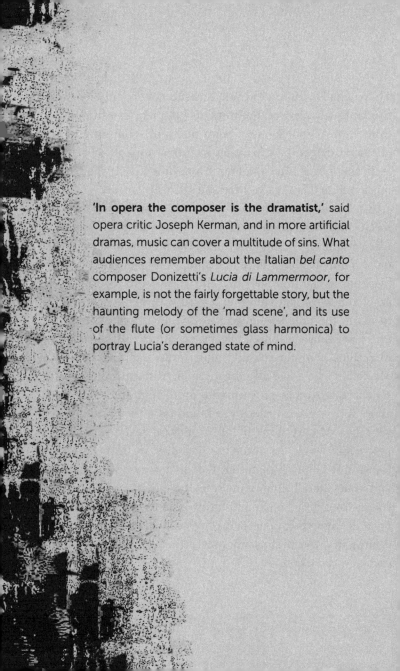

'In opera the composer is the dramatist,' said opera critic Joseph Kerman, and in more artificial dramas, music can cover a multitude of sins. What audiences remember about the Italian *bel canto* composer Donizetti's *Lucia di Lammermoor*, for example, is not the fairly forgettable story, but the haunting melody of the 'mad scene', and its use of the flute (or sometimes glass harmonica) to portray Lucia's deranged state of mind.

Music enables Mozart to deliver the plot, the motivation and the subtext of this highly complex scene simultaneously – a minor musical miracle – yet these can be found on every page of the score of *Figaro*. They can also be found at the other end of the scale in the epic drama of mature Verdi, whose penultimate opera *Otello* (*see* pages 120–1) is a perfect example of what great music can add to an already supreme drama. Without seeming rushed, the opera squeezes in every important element of the play while still leaving space for a passionate, lyrical love duet between Otello and Desdemona. Music allows Verdi to telescope time, shrinking it to speed up the action and then stretching it out so that we may linger over the passion of the protagonists. No wonder that there are those who consider the opera, as storytelling, to be a substantial improvement on Shakespeare's original.

THE ARIA AND DRAMA IN 3-D

Speaking of time, music's unique ability to tinker with it lies behind the survival of opera's most durable invention – the aria. Literally translating as 'song', it is the musical equivalent of the soliloquy in Elizabethan and Jacobean drama. Like Hamlet's 'to be or not to be', it is the route to a character's inner self.

By the time of Ibsen and Strindberg, the soliloquy had virtually disappeared from straight theatre, yet the aria still

OPERATIC FORMS

In the 18th century, **opera seria** (*see* page 53) and its comic cousin **opera buffa** were the dominant opera models, with the narrative delivered in recitative – sung dialogue – and moments of high emotion provided by strictly choreographed aria structures that were designed to allow soloists the opportunity to show off the technical prowess of their voices.

Although other forms of opera using spoken dialogue including the German *Singspiel* and the French *opéra comique*, did exist, it wasn't until the arrival of Mozart that opera would break free of the restrictions of these highly structured forms, moving beyond simple vocal exhibitionism and towards the expression of drama.

plays an essential role in opera. Swifter and more flexible than speech, it can let us into the inner world of a character simply by delivering a change of pace – acting as interior monologue, emotional confession, statement of intent or, sometimes, all three at once.

More than anything, though, an aria can provide a three-dimensional portrait of a character even when that character can hardly put their feelings into words. Tchaikovsky achieves this brilliantly in his much-loved opera *Eugene Onegin*. In the Pushkin verse novel on which it is based, the young heroine Tatyana can barely describe her adolescent passion for the distant and brooding Onegin. In the opera, when she writes the letter revealing her infatuation, Tchaikovsky frames it in a heart-breaking melody. This is exactly what we expect – except that the aria is twice interrupted. The composer is playing with our expectations just as Onegin is toying with Tatyana. When her big romantic melody is left unresolved, we experience Tatyana's own irresolution. Tchaikovsky does this more than once, the hesitant, tender tune is replaced by a more confident musical phrase to express Tatyana's renewed determination to confess everything to Onegin. However, this is also left incomplete. Only when the composer introduces a third, faster and more rhythmic melody is Tatyana's fate sealed. While there is no shortage of words in this 15-minute aria, for the most part of its heavenly length it is the music that is doing all the work.

This is what we mean when we say that the composer is the dramatist. When we think of the drama that unfolds at Figaro's wedding, it is Mozart's elegant and ambiguous melodies we remember, while Verdi's Cyprus in which the Moor's tragedy is played out is a place of flickering woodwind and violent brass. In each case the music does not simply accompany the drama, it completes and seals it. In *Onegin*, this is literally the case. After Tatyana despatches her letter, dawn rises to the sound of an oboe, this time playing a dancing folk melody. We are in the rural Russia where Tatyana has grown up and where she has tasted love for the first time. To reinforce this, Tchaikovsky ends the scene with one last repetition of the theme with which it began. As an audience, we find ourselves both inside and outside Tatyana's soul.

Once again, only opera can achieve this. This is not to imply that opera is in some way superior to straight drama, but it is unquestionably more three-dimensional. It is that third dimension which we enter when words, music and action combine and the whole is greater than the sum of its parts. It is what makes opera different.

'If music in general is an imitation of history, opera in particular is an imitation of human willfulness; it is rooted in the fact that we not only have feelings but insist upon having them at whatever cost to ourselves. The quality common to all the great operatic roles – Don Giovanni, Norma, Lucia, Tristan, Isolde, Brünnhilde – is that each of them is a passionate and willful state of being.'

W. H. Auden

LA BOHÈME
GIACOMO PUCCINI

With its perfect balance of realism and romanticism, comedy and pathos, *La Bohème* is one of the most popular operas in the canon. Yet the genesis of Puccini's intensely poignant opera – loosely based on Henri Murger's novel *Scènes de la Vie de Bohème*, along with memories of the composer's own student days – was not without controversy. Another composer, Ruggero Leoncavallo, was already working on a version of the story, and there was much rivalry and dissension between the two. Both were staged and Leoncavallo's had some initial success, although it was soon thoroughly overshadowed by Puccini's version, which premiered in Turin at the Teatro Regio, conducted by the young Arturo Toscanini (*see* page 113).

Filled with vibrant, bewitching and passionate music, Act I contains the opera's best-known arias – a sequence beginning with the poet Rodolfo's *'Che gelida manina'* answered by the seamstress Mimi's *'Si mi chiamano Mimi'* and culminating in the ensuing duet *'O soave fanciulla'* – which shows the pair becoming acquainting

- Four acts
- First performed 1896
- Libretto by Luigi Illica and Giuseppe Giacosa

and falling head-over-heels in love. The richly melodic score builds to Act III's lengthy scene at the city gates, featuring a showstopping quartet and ending with Mimi's sad farewell to Rodolfo ('*Addio. Donde lieta usci*'), demonstrating Puccini's genius as a musical dramatist. Crammed with recurring character themes, its famous music has not been to everyone's taste, however, with Benjamin Britten declaring himself 'sickened' by its 'cheapness and emptiness'.

Frequently updated – having been taken to the Paris of the 1930s and 1950s (by Jonathan Miller for ENO and Baz Luhrmann for Opera Australia respectively) as well as being transported to 1980s America via the musical *Rent* – *La Bohème* has a reputation for being an absolutely fail-safe piece. With its relatively small cast and numerous intimate scenes, it also works very well when spirited out of the grand opera house into more intimate environments, with notable productions taking place in small theatres, and even pubs, in recent years.

2 MYTHS AND LEGENDS: A FEW THINGS THAT OPERA IS NOT

Even when we have begun to understand opera's unique fascination, there is still a mountain of prejudice to overcome. Opera has always drawn on myths and legends for its subject matter and it has attracted plenty of hostile ones of its own, most of them inaccurate. Some of them, like Doctor Johnson's famous judgment about it being exotic and irrational, arise from unfamiliarity. Others are related to what people assume is its extravagant cost. Some tall tales are spread around by the popular media – often in tabloid headlines accusing companies of waste and mismanagement. Then there are the myths circulated by television and movies like the Marx Brothers' *A Night at the Opera*, where every soprano is built like a hippopotamus. So before we explore some of opera's most memorable moments, it may help to engage in some gentle myth-busting...

MYTH 1: OPERA IS EXPENSIVE AND INACCESSIBLE

Not necessarily. Of course opera began as an extravagant public spectacle to parade the prosperity of the elite, but almost immediately cheaper alternatives became available. The elaborate Italian operas of Handel's time competed with ballad operas like *The Beggar's Opera* which mingled popular tunes and spoken dialogue. Mozart wrote Italian operas for

Vienna but he also wrote crowd-pleasing musical dramas like *The Magic Flute* for the city's cheaper theatres. In France, grand opera lived cheek by jowl with *opéras comiques* like Jacques Offenbach's *La Belle Hélène*, as well as the ever-popular melodrama *Carmen*. While in the Berlin of the 1920s, Bertolt Brecht and Kurt Weill's *The Threepenny Opera* was stuffed with popular songs, as was George Gershwin's *Porgy and Bess*.

In our own time, small-scale companies have grown up to introduce new audiences to opera in slimmed-down productions that do not require a second mortgage to purchase tickets. Opera has also moved outside of the confines of the prestigious opera houses themselves, with works popping up in pubs, shops and even abandoned swimming pools, while the major opera companies are now broadcasting their performances to cinema screens across the globe.

MYTH 2: OPERA IS INCOMPREHENSIBLE

This is a misunderstanding. It is true that until the 19th century, almost all opera was sung in Italian and occasionally in French. However, most of the best-loved operas of Verdi, Puccini, Wagner and Strauss were created in the language of their audiences. This was equally true of Russia and Central Europe. Even when opera was presented in a foreign language, from the very beginning audiences often followed with a libretto –

OPERA AND THE STATE

Since the war, with the exception of a handful of rich American and Far Eastern houses, only the state has been able to afford to produce traditional opera on a regular basis. As a result, opera has proved itself extremely flexible, successfully adapting to new financial constraints.

In the 1920s, 30s and 40s Igor Stravinsky, Maurice Ravel and Benjamin Britten frequently wrote for a few singers supported by a handful of musicians. Today many composers (and certainly their financial backers) prefer working in small theatres, while in our more cost-conscious world, operatic classics such as *Carmen*, *Don Giovanni* and even Wagner's 15-hour *Ring Cycle* have also all been presented successfully in reduced versions.

the equivalent of modern day surtitles. And there were always exceptions. In Germany, until recently, opera was often sung in translation, just as it is at English National Opera. Today, there is no difficulty following opera in an unfamiliar language, as almost every house has surtitles.

MYTH 3: THE PLOTS ARE IMPOSSIBLE TO UNDERSTAND

Not all of them, and far more is made of incomprehensible plots than should be. It is certainly true that much early Italian opera was drawn from distant Greek myths or complicated Renaissance tales, but the plot was never the prime purpose of these early works – in Italy, audiences came mainly for the singers, for example, while in France they were drawn by dance and scenic spectacle.

But even as early as the 1780s, storytelling began to take precedence, with the supreme combination of Mozart and his librettist da Ponte producing subtle and humane comedies such as *The Marriage of Figaro* or *Così Fan Tutte*, the likes of which can challenge the plays of Chekhov or Ayckbourn for psychological truth. Consequently, most of Verdi and Wagner's mature operas are fairly easy to follow, while by the time we reach the operas of Richard Strauss or Leoš Janáček, we could well be watching modern drama in musical dress.

In the USA today, many operas like André Previn's *A Streetcar Named Desire* are based on popular movies or – like John Adams' *The Death of Klinghoffer* – derive from contemporary television reportage.

MYTH 4: OPERA SINGERS ARE FAT, UNGAINLY AND UNSUITED TO THEIR ROMANTIC ROLES

Not any longer. And not at the very beginning either. In the 17th and 18th centuries, some of the most popular sopranos started their careers as slender and charming teenagers. It was only when the accompanying orchestral textures became heavier that singers were advised that they should put on weight to combat the sound coming from the orchestra pit. In fact, even that proved to be largely an exaggeration. This particular myth was busted by Maria Callas, who undertook a very public diet and reinvented her entire image. The overweight diva has now become a thing of the past.

FEUDS AND FACTIONS

Tales of warring divas and their rivalries have also passed into operatic myth – feuds which have captured the imagination of the public as well as fuelled the creative fires, and commercial appeal, of the performers themselves, even if their scale and intensity may often have been exaggerated.

In 1727 the Italian sopranos Francesca Cuzzoni and Faustina Bordoni came to blows while singing on stage in London, with bookings for both ladies soaring as a result. Dame Nellie Melba famously barred Italian rival Luisa Tetrazzini from performing at Covent Garden for many years, Tetrazzini (whom Melba habitually referred to as 'that dwarf') only having the opportunity to debut while Melba was in Australia and unable to intervene. In the mid-20th century sopranos Maria Callas and Renata Tebaldi nurtured a great public feud, with one British newspaper quoting Callas as declaring that to compare herself with Tebaldi would be 'like comparing champagne with cognac. No – champagne with Coca-Cola!'

THE TURN OF THE SCREW
BENJAMIN BRITTEN

Based on the novella by Henry James, *The Turn of the Screw* relays the attempts of a nameless governess to save the children in her care – Miles and Flora – from the ghosts of their former governess Miss Jessel, and Peter Quint, a servant in the house who was suspected of exercising a sinister influence over them. One of the most admired post-war operas and the result of a commission for the Venice Biennale in 1954, it is a chamber work, written to be performed with an ensemble of 13 players rather than a full orchestra, and intended to be easily taken on tour and performed in a variety of small performance spaces.

Deeply unsettling from the outset, with the prologue Britten establishes a haunting theme that underpins the opera and returns in 15 variations serving to link one scene to the next, each acting as a further 'turn of the screw'. Additional spookiness is provided by the chilling use of innocent nursery songs, prayer book chants and Latin mnemonics, all of which serve to contrast with the

- Two acts
- First performed 1954
- Libretto by Myfanwy Piper
  after Henry James' 1898 story

music associated with the governess which is stark, percussive and neurotic, reflecting her hysterical paranoia. Threaded throughout are the ghost's hypnotic vocal lines that call out to the children as the opera builds towards its powerful climax, the final battle for Miles' soul. The opera is renowned for the difficult vocal demands it places on its young singers — Miles must be sung by a treble although Flora is often played by a young adult soprano, as very few children are capable of singing it convincingly.

With its tightly controlled scenes and gripping music, *The Turn of the Screw* marked a point of departure for Britten musically. After it, chamber opera would become his primary concern, while his use of Schoenberg's twelve-tone technique as demonstrated in the opera — a method of musical composition ensuring that all 12 notes of the chromatic scale are sounded as often as one another without being in key — would become his central technique for achieving intensity.

3

WHERE TO START:
CLOSE ENCOUNTERS
OF THE OPERATIC KIND

There is no substitute for the experience of hearing a complete work in an opera house. However, despite moves to improve the situation (*see* pages 134–143) opera tickets are often expensive and sometimes inaccessible outside major cities. For those who have missed an early encounter with live opera, the most common points of entry are its arias and excerpts, which are readily available on home audio and video or the host of operatic websites.

From the very beginning, audiences have been captivated by individual moments that distil the whole character of an opera into a few intense minutes. Indeed, in 16th century Italy or later in Georgian England, celebrated performers would arrange concerts combining favourite arias, duets and scenes to satisfy the taste of inexperienced listeners without challenging their short attention spans. Today, for those who are nervous of exposing themselves to three hours of musical drama, there are many ways to discover the quintessence of opera. What follows is a selection of moments from the key composers and works that still pack out our opera houses.

PUCCINI

No composer was more skilled in placing an aria at exactly the right moment to release the build-up of emotional tension than Giacomo Puccini (1858–1924). In *Tosca*, just as the sinister police chief Scarpia is about to force a sexual bargain on the eponymous prima donna, she pours her despair into the aria *'Vissi d'Arte'* – a plea for pity and respect that has become the calling card of all great divas. Maria Callas made this her signature tune, and sopranos have tried to equal her ever since. *'Nessun Dorma'*, which became inextricably bound up with football during the World Cup in Italy in 1990, occupies a crucial moment in Puccini's opera *Turandot* when the tenor hero confronts the savage kingdom that the icy princess has created to punish the treacherous male sex. Less well-known but even greater than these is the quartet in the third act of *La Bohème* where the tubercular heroine and her poet lover are briefly reconciled, while their friends, the painter Marcello and the *grisette* Musetta, scream abuse at each other and break up for the umpteenth time – a telling combination of tenderness and irony that only Mozart has bettered.

VERDI

During his long career, Giuseppe Verdi (1813–1901) grew from a creator of popular potboilers to the subtlest and most powerful of all Italian opera composers. In his early maturity, he wrote three masterpieces combining psychological truth, unforgettable melody and vocal splendour. Gilda's graceful aria *'Caro Nome'* in *Rigoletto* demonstrates Verdi's lyrical gift at its most sensitive, even though her declaration of love is directed at an exploitative womanizer. However, the most characteristic arias in the opera belong to the hunchback hero himself whose bitterness finds vivid expression in *'Pari Siamo'* and *'Cortigiani'*. The opera is built on the solid foundations of a great classic, Hugo's *Le Roi S'amuse*.

If Verdi's unique affinity for great literature appeals, his adaptation of Schiller's massive *Don Carlo* contains a blood-chilling duet in Act III between King Philip II and the fearsome Grand Inquisitor. An even more celebrated literary work *La Dame aux Camélias (The Lady of the Camelias)* provided the narrative for Verdi's most popular opera of this period, *La Traviata*, in which Violetta's death scene and the aria *'Addio del Passato'* showcase the composer at his heart-breaking best.

MOZART

It may seem a huge leap from the Mediterranean passion of Verdi to the Rococo elegance of Wolfgang Amadeus Mozart (1756–1791) but the Italian and the Austrian have more in common than might initially appear to be the case. Both composers take artificial forms such as duets, trios and larger ensembles and fill them with subtle psychology. The scene in *Le Nozze di Figaro* where the Countess and her maid Susanna attempt to hide the lustful page-boy Cherubino from the jealous Count combines sensuality and farce in a fashion that has never been surpassed. Mozart's gift for fusing sentiment and cynicism is even more vividly embodied in the quintet *'Di Scrivermi'* in *Così Fan Tutte*. On the surface a tender farewell between two girls and their fiancés departing to the wars, underneath each of the protagonists is lying – either to each other or to themselves.

For even deeper darkness, the black comedy of *Don Giovanni* possesses a uniquely manic energy. The catalogue aria *'Madamina'* where Giovanni's manservant Leporello reveals his master's many thousands of previous conquests is justly celebrated, while the scene in which the statue of the murdered Commendatore arrives in Giovanni's palace to accept his invitation to dinner and drag him down to hell is utterly arresting.

WAGNER

At the other end of the scale from Mozart's shapely comedies sit the massive four-hour-plus edifices of Richard Wagner (1813–83). Because Wagner's great achievement was to weave a seamless musical fabric over many hours, it is almost impossible to take a pair of scissors and cut off a representative slice. This hasn't stopped people from trying, however – ever since his music became a Europe-wide obsession in the second half of the 19th century, interpreters have tried to extract sections. The English conductor Sir Thomas Beecham sourly described them as 'bleeding chunks'.

EARLY OPERATIC ENCOUNTERS

The right opera presented in the right way can captivate even the youngest audiences, and the earlier the encounter the better. Two classic masterpieces remain supreme starting points and never fail to cast their spell.

Although not written for children, Mozart's *Magic Flute* fuses the emotional journey of two young lovers with the pantomime knockabout of their companions. It has moments of spiritual profundity but remains childlike both in its transparent musical score and its wide-eyed fairy tale narrative, and has inspired many new generations of opera-goers. Janáček's *The Cunning Little Vixen* (*see* pages 142–3) might seem more challenging to a child but it is equally enthralling. This tale of a young fox cub who escapes from captivity into the wild has its fair proportion of heartless cruelty, but then, so do most children! I have seen a family audience of 2,000 silenced by the arrival of the grown-up Vixen's brood of cubs set to a rhythmic motif, which, once heard, haunts the ears for weeks.

While we can hardly call them arias, a few monologues hint at the grandeur of the whole. Lohengrin's narration, *'In Fernem Land'*, where he reveals his mysterious legendary origins, has the translucency that characterizes the complete opera. In his reflective monologue *'Wahn, Wahn'*, the humane cobbler-poet Hans Sachs in *Die Meistersinger* reveals much of the opera's warmer side before it opens out into a huge nationalistic pageant. There is no more sensitive moment in the entire 15 hours of the *Ring Cycle* than Siegmund's ecstatic hymn to Spring *'Winterstürme'*, which leads into the most heartfelt (albeit incestuous) love duet in all Wagner. However, none of these give a real sense of the whole. For contrast, it may be best to sample the rapturous *'Liebestod'*, which concludes *Tristan und Isolde* as the lovers sink erotically into oblivion, or Wotan's previously mentioned farewell to his daughter, particularly as in the latter the surrounding magic fire is conjured up by a brilliantly coloured orchestra of more than 100 musicians.

ONE-OFFS

Wagner, Puccini and Verdi were professional opera composers and wrote little else. Mozart's catalogue contains every kind of music imaginable but his half-dozen mature operas were almost certainly closest to his heart. Other great composers – notably Rossini, Berlioz and Strauss – have left a huge legacy which is probably best approached when you have fallen under the spell of their predecessors. However, there are a few stand-alone masterpieces that have achieved both popularity and the highest critical regard. Together with the works of Mozart, Puccini and Verdi mentioned above, they are known in the business as 'the bankers' – operas that are depended upon to fill seats when times are tough. Most popular of these is Georges Bizet's *Carmen*, closely followed by the double bill of *Cavelleria Rusticana* by Pietro Mascagni and *I Pagliacci* by Ruggero Leoncavallo (known together colloquially as 'Cav and Pag'). All three of these are based on boulevard melodramas, which might explain their success.

Carmen's arias have delighted popular audiences for a century and a half, not only as showpieces for great singers but also reconceived in a host of styles from big band jazz to heavy rock. The scene in which Carmen and her gypsy companions cut cards to tell their futures (*'Melons! Coupons!'*) is gripping drama characteristic of the work as a whole. *Cavelleria Rusticana* is exactly the kind of popular drama that filled the theatres of Italy's provinces before the arrival of cinema. The Easter hymn (*'Regina Coeli, Laetare'*) which appears early in the opera's action, pays homage to traditional Catholic choral music, while grafting on to it the popular appeal of Neapolitan song. *I Pagliacci* is just as cleverly crafted and even more vivid, and contains one aria *'Vesti la Giubba'* for the tragic clown Pagliacco that has introduced whole generations and some of opera's most celebrated tenors – from Enrico Caruso to Plácido Domingo – to Italian opera.

Ludwig van Beethoven's *Fidelio* was also commissioned by a popular theatre, this time the Theater am Kärntnertor in Vienna. Here the resemblance with Carmen and 'Cav and Pag' ends. The politically radical Beethoven was inspired by this tale of tyranny and the struggle for freedom to write some of his most inspired music. The scene where the political prisoner Florestan is rescued by his wife (*'Gott Welch Dunkel hier'*) is a thrilling piece of miniature music drama and reveals how much Beethoven influenced the music of successors like Wagner and Strauss.

WHERE NEXT?

After these operatic pinnacles you have a broad range of choices. You can dig deeper into the repertoire you have already encountered. You have 20 Mozart operas, 13 Puccinis and 29 Verdis to choose from. Wagner's 14 works will probably take up even more of your time. If that sounds too exhausting, you can explore predecessors and successors. Between Mozart and early Verdi comes the Italian composer Gioacchino Rossini, whose *Barber of Seville*, a fizzy and tuneful comedy, almost equals the works of Mozart and Puccini as a crowd-puller. Other Italian comic operas such as Gaetano Donizetti's *Don Pasquale* and Vincenzo Bellini's *L'Elisir d'Amore* wait in the wings. The latter two composers were also popular as creators of high drama, exploiting the vocal fireworks of great divas in a florid style that became known as *bel canto*.

OPERATIC SPECTACLE

From its origins, opera married vocal display with prodigious theatrical spectacle. Early Italian operas boasted sea battles and transformation scenes that would put a Broadway musical to shame, while by the turn of the 20th century grand opera was offering everything lovers of wide-screen cinema might wish for.

However, for opera's most thrilling spectacles you must turn eastwards to the historical dramas of the Russian Empire. Russian imperial opera commandeered the country's many massive male choirs to swell the stage action in the nationalistic epics of Modest Mussorgsky, Alexander Borodin and Nikolai Rimsky-Korsakov. In pride of place is the coronation scene from Mussorgsky's *Boris Godunov*, where the Tsar is welcomed with massed choruses, as many extras as the theatre can muster and a tintinnabulation of cathedral bells.

Wagner is sandwiched between early Romantic German operas such as Carl von Weber's ghostly *Der Freischütz* and the legions of later works influenced by him. Dominating these are the operas of Richard Strauss. If you have a strong stomach, there are his two terrifying early one-act dramas – the sleazy and decadent *Salome* and the violent and disturbing Greek tragedy *Elektra*, both with libretti by his regular collaborator, the poet Hugo von Hofmannstahl. Composer and author also joined forces for Strauss's most popular work *Der Rosenkavalier*, which dresses up a Mozartian plot in late Romantic musical clothes. Containing the bewitching trio *'Marie Theres'*, the final scene, where the fairly mature Marschallin surrenders her teenage lover to a girl closer to his own age, never fails to touch and delight.

If spectacle's your thing, then you should turn your head towards the works of the grand Russian operas (*see* pages 77–8), while in our own century there is a legion of works by Claude Debussy, Leoš Janáček, Alban Berg, George Gershwin and Benjamin Britten which combine the lyric intensity of the great Puccini and Wagner operas with a psychological realism more suited to the age of Ibsen and Chekhov. They are all surprisingly accessible but by now you may feel in need of a little background and context. Opera grew and developed from its origins in 16th century Italy in a twisted line full of knots and switchbacks, but its history offers a great deal to explain the oddities of this 'exotic and irrational entertainment'.

CARMEN
GEORGES BIZET

Now one of the world's most beloved operas, Bizet's masterpiece *Carmen* was far from an overnight success. Adapted from a short story by Prosper Mérimée, its blatant sexuality and risqué morality were considered shocking and obscene to its conservative audience at its Parisian premiere. Tragically, Bizet would die during its opening run under the impression that it was a failure, yet it was only a few years, however, before audiences across the globe were won over by the opera's Spanish feel, compelling characters, richly coloured choruses and bewitching melodies.

While *Carmen* is described as an *opéra comique* it is also a highly original work, containing an emotional realism not seen before in opera. And while it is full of dazzling, vibrant music that has now become part of the general consciousness, such as the *Toreador Song* of Act II *('Votre toast, je peux vous le rendre')*, beneath the exuberance lie hints of its tragic dénouement. It is also very much a vehicle for a diva, requiring as it does exceptional acting and singing talents from its lead – while the rest of the cast, including

- Four acts
- First performed 1873
- Libretto by Henri Meilhac and Ludovic Halévy based on the short story by Prosper Mérimée

matador Escamillo, peasant girl Micaëla, and corporal Don José all have fine arias, there is no disputing that the passionate gypsy Carmen is the star of this show. Originally written for the small, light voice of the mezzo-soprano Célestine Galli-Marie (with whom it was believed Bizet was having an affair during rehearsals), it has also been sung successfully by regular sopranos, including Maria Callas and Emma Calvé.

Productions of *Carmen* number in the thousands and its sheer ubiquity has left it ripe for reimagining, with many producers transferring the action to other 20th century working settings. It has also been adapted more radically – most notably as *Carmen Jones*, Oscar Hammerstein's 1943 musical comedy with an African-American story set in a southern military base – as well as being the subject of many film treatments. Testament to its ability to transcend its 19th century French origins, *Carmen* remains one of the only works from this period to have withstood the test of time. Its enduring popularity shows no signs of waning.

4

WHOSE OPERA
IS IT ANYWAY?
A BRIEF HISTORY

Opera is infinitely adaptable. The same word can describe Henry Purcell's *Dido and Aeneas*, premiered in a 17th century London girls' school with just a handful of singers, or a cast of 100 Italian performers re-enacting a riot in the Council Chamber of Renaissance Genoa in Giuseppe Verdi's *Simon Boccanegra*.

Only one factor tends to be constant – as a public entertainment, requiring accomplished singers and musicians let alone elaborate sets and costumes – opera has never been really cheap. Indeed, one commentator has made the sardonic observation that there has only been one important question in the history of opera, 'Who pays the deficit?' From the Italian courts to the state opera houses of our own day, composers have always had to adapt to available resources and the tastes and preferences of whoever paid for them. As a result, the history of opera is usually the history of who owned it.

If composers are clever enough they can manipulate a patron into picking up the tab – sometimes mortgaging an entire kingdom in support of an epic project such as Richard Wagner's *Ring Cycle*. For most of its history though, opera has been owned by the most powerful in society and the singers and impressarios whose skills they retained to please their friends and contemporaries.

EARLY TIMES

In Renaissance Italy during the early 16th century, power and patronage belonged to the leading courtly families. When they celebrated a wedding uniting two great dynasties, there were extended periods of feasting interspersed with dramatic entertainments known as *intermedi*.

As the century wore on, patrons became more ambitious in their theatrical demands – at the top end of the scale, the Medici wedding of 1589 in Florence boasted elaborate visual drama and a full score by the city's most famous composer, Jacopo Peri. Among the guests at a later Medici wedding were their competitors, the Gonzaga family of Mantua, and very possibly their new composer-in-residence, Claudio Monteverdi. It was this meeting of power, money, spectacle and great musical genius which jump-started the history of opera.

ITALY: THE BIRTHPLACE OF OPERA

When Monteverdi's *Orfeo* received its premiere at the Gonzaga Court in Mantua in 1607, the word 'opera' did not even exist. The composer called his creation a *favola per musica* – a musical fable. Francesco Gonzaga commissioned the piece to impress his artistic circle of friends. To ensure his success, he imported the star singer from Peri's triumph in Florence, solo choristers and an extravagant ensemble of more than 30 musicians and singers. The most striking aspect of the world's first ever opera was that it only received two performances and then disappeared from the repertory for 300 years. Francesco's purpose was not to leave a musical legacy to the future but to score a spectacular coup in the present.

It did, however, turn Monteverdi into one of the most sought-after composers in Europe. After conquering Venice with his *Vespers of 1610*, Monteverdi secured the post of music director at Saint Mark's cathedral in Venice, Italy's most prosperous city-state. Its wealthy audience of traders and entrepreneurs demanded festivals of opera during the city's Carnival season, and theatres sprung up all over the city to cater for their tastes.

In his final years, Monteverdi composed the two most durable operas of the early Italian baroque, *Il Ritorno d'Ulisse (The Return of Ulysses)*, with its classical narrative told through a series of ravishing solo arias, and *L'Incoronazione di Poppea (The Coronation of Poppea)*, drawn from history rather than legend and dramatizing the scurrilous tale of the emperor Nero's murderous passion for his mistress Poppea. The latter's enthralling combination of high passion and sardonic observation has ensured Monteverdi's continued presence in the operatic repertory for more than three and a half centuries after his death.

OPERA SERIA

The prevailing opera model for much of the 17th and 18th centuries was *opera seria*, also frequently called Neapolitan opera – an Italian style based upon the conventions of the High Baroque era which was produced not only in Italy but also Spain, Austria, England and the German states. The narrative was recounted in recitative, which advanced the dramatic action, and arias, which reflected a character's emotions.

A distinctive characteristic of the form was its *da capo* aria structure, with its ABA form, where the first section (A) is repeated after the B section, but with improvised embellishments. *Opera seria* composers include the Neapolitan Niccolò Jommelli and Handel, whose *Rinaldo* is seen as a particular high-water mark for the style.

L'INCORONAZIONE DI POPPEA (THE CORONATION OF POPPEA)
CLAUDIO MONTEVERDI

Monteverdi's last opera (and quite possibly his last work altogether), *L'Incoronazione di Poppea* is believed to be the first opera to be based on a historical rather than a mythological or fictional subject. Two copies of the score have survived from Monteverdi's time, and the differences between them and the existing versions of the libretto have raised questions about the authenticity of the music they contain. It is now believed that some sections, including the music for Poppea's love interest Ottone, along with the final duet between the Emperor Nerone and Poppea, were written by younger composers such as Benedetto Ferrari, among others.

More lightly orchestrated than Monteverdi's other operas *Orfeo* or *Il Ritorno d'Ulisse (The Return of Ulysses)*, *Poppea* is close to the ideal of a 'sung play' in which the drama is continuous and each character is sharply rendered. The opera premiered during Carnival in Venice, when licence to push moral boundaries was freer than it would have been usually. The libretto, drawn from the biographical portraits of the Ancient Romans Tacitus and

- Prologue and three acts
- First performed 1643
- Libretto by Giovanni Busenello

Suetonius, is an exploration of adultery, lust and ambition, while the score manages to run the gamut of emotions, fears and desires. Featuring a large cast of 28 singing characters, including seven ensemble parts, the music contains a number of exquisite lyrical passages such as the lullaby with which the nurse Arnalta calms Poppea *('Addaggiati Poppea')* and the loving duet between Poppea and Nerone *('Non più s'interporrà noia o dimora')*, as well as numerous scenes that burn with erotic energy.

Having been largely forgotten as a composer of opera, Monteverdi's works were only rediscovered at the end of the 19th-century, and performances of *Poppea* were rare until the 1960s and the quartercentenary of the composer's birth. It is not hard to see why the work has become so popular in recent years, however – whether playing up the cynical erotic decadence of Nerone's court or its hazy moral compass and maze of motive and emotion, *Poppea* remains an astonishingly modern, hard-hitting opera.

FRANCE: OPERA, GLORIFIED

Opera travelled to France by the same route as cuisine – when Catherine di Medici married the heir to the French throne, she arrived surrounded by both Italian chefs and musicians. Though if gastronomy rooted itself swiftly, opera took rather longer. The French nation was paralyzed by civil and religious wars for much of the first half of the 17th century and it was only with the establishment of a centralized court in Versailles that France began to develop its own unique form of lyric theatre. Like everything else in the country, this was designed to reflect the glory of the monarchy. In Versailles, Fontainebleau and the grand Parisian Palais Royal, opera was the property of the Sun King Louis XVI himself.

Louis' musical tastes were largely dictated by the Italian composer Giovanni Batista Lulli. Swiftly changing his name to the more French spelling of Lully, he soon established a Royal Academy of Music to match the literary one that already boasted the likes of Molière and Racine among its ranks. The version of opera that Lully developed here could not have been more different from the Italian lyric theatre that inspired it. Lully's *tragédies lyriques* were essentially extended ballets occasionally invaded by fragments of musical drama. In time, Lully's successor Jean-Philippe Rameau took personal control of French baroque opera, producing no fewer than 32 lyric dramas, ranging from his debut tragedy *Hippolyte et Aricie* to the comedy *Platée*, a sad and funny tale of a vain and ugly nymph which appeals greatly to contemporary tastes. Yet during Rameau's long career, elaborate dance, melody and spectacle continued to hold sway in Paris, with dramatic storytelling remaining in the margins.

ENGLAND: AN EARLY INTRODUCTION

Meanwhile, opera as we would recognize it today was finding its natural home in London, thanks to a German trained in Italy. In 1714, there was no heir to the English throne and the crown passed to the House of Hanover. The new King George I spoke hardly a word of English but he understood Italian and loved that country and its music. When he arrived to take up the throne, London had already fallen under the sway of a prodigious young Saxon composer with Italian musical tastes called Georg Frideric Haendel. Within 40 years, and now a British citizen with his name Anglicized to Handel, he had transformed every aspect of music in England, most particularly opera. In his birthplace of Halle, Handel had devoured all the German and Italian music available, topping up his studies with visits to Rome, Naples, Florence and particularly Venice. Barely 26 but already a formidable networker, he was commissioned by the Queen's Theatre in London's Haymarket to write a new Italian opera. Throwing together left-over fragments from previous works and brand new arias, it took him less than a month to compose *Rinaldo*. In a society in love with novelty it was an overnight sell-out success.

During the early 1700s London was the most commercially advanced city in the world. Apart from its importance as a centre of trade, it also had a burgeoning entertainment industry. Several English composers, principally Henry Purcell and Thomas Arne, had already created lyric theatre works such as *King Arthur* that were much closer to musical pageant than opera as we now know it, and which reached a wide popular audience. However, the taste for imported Italian opera was particularly well developed and a rich and well-travelled clientele demanded the kind of music and drama they had enjoyed in Italy. Like everything else in London, producing opera was a high-risk venture and, time after time, the opera seasons in the Haymarket failed to cover their costs. However, the city remained a magnet for Europe's finest performers, and Handel's output benefited from the talents of great Italian divas and the stratospheric voices of castratos (*see* page 100), who were the pop legends of their day. The only threats to the continuing dominance of Italian opera in London were British politics and religion.

The House of Hanover was strictly Protestant. People could still recall the religious conflicts of the previous generation and anything associated with the Catholic Church was regarded with deep suspicion. Within a decade of the triumph of *Rinaldo*, Italian opera seasons were suspended and despite later attempts to revive them, home-grown musical theatre like John Gay's *Beggar's Opera*, with its staunchly English text and populist satirical edge, now held pride of place. Ever the pragmatist, Handel switched his attention to oratorio in the English language, creating works like *Jephtha* and *Samson* with large choruses and ensembles that in many respects were even more operatic than his operas. Towards the end of his life he composed *Semele* in English, combining the best of both genres, but it was another hundred years before opera in English returned to London.

DIDO AND AENEAS
HENRY PURCELL

The only major piece of music theatre in English before the operas of Benjamin Britten in the 20th century, *Dido and Aeneas* is a monumental Baroque work and can be seen as England's operatic crowning glory. Purcell's first and only all-sung 'true' opera, it appears to have been initially performed at Josias Priest's Boarding School for girls in 1689. After 1705 it disappeared as a staged work, with only sporadic concert performances, until 1895 – with the first staged version of modern times at the Lyceum Theatre to mark the bicentenary of Purcell's death.

Sadly the earliest surviving score in existence dates from after 1777, some 90 years after the opera was composed, and the prologue and the end of the second act have been lost, while the authorship of certain parts of the score has been questioned. *Dido and Aeneas'* elliptical libretto, the only existing 17th century source, has also been criticized by some – highly condensed in nature, it is notable for its underdevelopment of the character of Aeneas, as well as

- Three acts
- First performed 1689
- Libretto by Nahum Tate

for leaving certain key events such as the manner of Dido's death unspecified. However, the quality of the music, which contains a wealth of richly charged and supple melody, and the human scale of the tragedy it conveys, go some way to making up for any such perceived shortcomings.

Integrating the dances favoured in French opera, and following Italian fashion by dwelling on arias, *Dido and Aeneas* breaks new ground with Purcell's treatment of lyrics. Based on the principle of a solo aria followed or answered by a chorus, the most substantial number comes in the final scene with Dido's lament. Here the Carthaginian queen's line, 'when I am laid in earth', is sung over a repeated phrase, the music alternately caressing and resisting the lyrics. With these impassioned yet plaintive final cries, Purcell achieves one of the great moments in opera, as tragic and heart rending as anything in Wagner or Verdi.

THE ARRIVAL OF CLASSICAL OPERA AND THE RISE OF GRAND OPERA

When Handel died in the mid-18th century, operatic style still varied according to national tastes and politics. In France it belonged to the King and Court; in England it was owned by commercial promoters, while in the central European Habsburg Empire Italian opera still dominated – although in a realm governed from Vienna speaking a cocktail of German and Slav languages, it was no longer the only game in town. Nor were serious musical dramas like Handel's the only diversions on offer. Popular Italian 'comic opera' (*opera buffa*) appealed to bourgeois Viennese audiences, and if they preferred their own German language, there was also the home-grown *Singspiel*, with spoken dialogue interrupted by stand-alone songs rather like a Broadway musical.

AUSTRIA: OPERA TRANSFORMED

During the mid- to late-18th century, opera's centre of gravity shifted from Italy and France towards Austria. France's most successful composer of serious operas, Christoph Willibald Gluck, chose to make his home in Vienna and was appointed court composer by the Emperor. His movement to reform opera, which began in the late 1750s and advocated putting dramatic action first and eschewing vocal virtuosity, music or dance for its own sake, resulted in grave masterpieces such as *Alceste*, *Orphée* and *Iphigénie*, which were hailed and imitated all over the continent.

But one man was to leave his mark on every variety of lyric theatre and, in doing, take opera in an entirely new direction. Wolfgang Amadeus Mozart composed the three greatest of all *opera buffas*, the two finest *Singspiels*, 13 *opera serias* and a handful of one-acters, all before his premature death in 1791 at the age of 37. It could only have happened in a great imperial cosmopolis like Vienna, where writing and theatrical talent were in ready supply.

One further element in Mozart's Viennese career changed not only the composer but operatic history itself. Unlike many other composers of the time who held court titles and privileges, Mozart was a freelance. Hopelessly constrained in Salzburg, he threw himself upon Vienna with a *Singspiel* especially created for the Emperor Joseph II himself. *Die Entführung aus dem Serail (The Abduction from the Seraglio)* was spiced up by being set in Ottoman Turkey, recently at war with the Empire. Its success, coupled with his collaboration with the librettist Lorenzo da Ponte, opened the door for his great operas *Le Nozze di Figaro (The Marriage of Figaro), Don Giovanni* and *Così Fan Tutte*, followed by the transcendent *Die Zauberflöte (The Magic Flute)*. Although Mozart died in debt, his operatic legacy was assured.

After Mozart, and by the end of the 18th century, post-revolutionary France was undergoing massive social upheaval and exporting it to Austria and across Europe. It found a sympathetic ear in Ludwig van Beethoven, a self-supporting freelance with a radical spirit, although still heavily dependent on aristocratic patrons. Trapped in Vienna when Napoleon Bonaparte besieged the city in 1807, the composer's only opera *Fidelio* – a rescue drama set in a prison in a police state – was written, rehearsed and performed under siege. In it Beethoven the political radical and Beethoven the symphonist merge to create music theatre that was to influence the world of opera for generations.

FRANCE: THE RISE OF GRAND OPERA

Despite being defeated by the alliance of Austria, Britain and Russia, France held great sway over the opera world during the first third of the 19th century. The restoration of the French monarchy opened the door to a wealthy new bourgeoisie with money to spend and the world's most glamorous (and now restored) city to spend it in.

To begin with, they turned to Italy's most prodigious opera composer Gioacchino Rossini. In Paris he exploited the new epic style he had been developing, writing biblical and historical epics including *The Siege of Corinth and Moses in Egypt*, which suited the well-heeled audiences who now called the tune in France. The high point of Rossini's Paris triumphs was his huge final opera *William Tell*.

DON GIOVANNI
WOLFGANG AMADEUS MOZART

Born as a morality tale and subsequently told many times in different ways, the story of the fictional libertine and seducer *Don Giovanni* has its ultimate theatrical source in a 17th century Spanish black farce by Tirso de Molina. Commissioned for Prague after the huge success there of *Le Nozze di Figaro (The Marriage of Figaro)*, for the libretto Mozart turned again to Lorenzo da Ponte, who took his story from an obscure one-act opera that had been recently presented in Venice. Billed as a *dramma giocoso* – a term denoting a mix of serious and comic action – da Ponte's clever script inspired Mozart's brilliant score, which lends macabre humour, Gothic spookiness and tragedy to the story of the promiscuous nobleman who escapes all retribution save death.

From the Gothic opening bars of the majestic overture which set the mood, through to the trombone blasts exclusively associated with the righteous vengeance of the Commendatore (whose statue ultimately drags the unrepentent seducer down to hell), musically *Don Giovanni* is the darkest-toned of Mozart's operas. It is also his

- Two acts
- First performed 1787
- Libretto by Lorenzo da Ponte

most ambiguous – Giovanni himself has long fascinated writers and philosophers, attracted by the impossibility of penetrating such a mercurial character, and Mozart's score deliberately reveals very little about his motivation. Possessing no long major arias and adapting to the style of each of whomever he is trying to seduce, his voice too is ambiguous. Singing neither high nor low, the role can be taken by a bass or baritone.

After its first production in Prague, Mozart revised the score for Vienna, writing a major additional aria *('Mi tradi')* for Elvira (a noble lady abandoned by Giovanni), a replacement aria for Don Ottavio (a gentleman betrothed to the Commendatore's daughter) and an additional duet for the peasant Zerlina and Giovanni's servant Leporello, along with other minor changes and cuts including the work's final moralizing scene. Productions today largely follow the Prague version, though tend to include the Vienna version's additional arias.

Other Italians such as Gaspare Spontini and Luigi Cherubini also helped to pave the way for the new style of *grand opéra*, with creations like *La Vestale* and *Lodoïska*, their stirring historical subjects fitting the requirements of this new form. Both were trumped, however, by the French composer Daniel Esprit Auber, whose *La Muette des Portici* – premiered at the Paris Opéra in 1828 – recounted a 17th century Neapolitan revolt against foreign invasion, reaching its climax with its heroine plunging into a volcano. In an extraordinary example of life imitating art, the opera's premiere in Brussels would provoke a revolutionary uprising which would later lead to Belgium's independence from the Netherlands.

However, grand opera in Paris was to be dominated not by a Frenchman but the German born Giacomo Meyerbeer. His masterpiece *Les Huguenots*, premiered in Paris in 1836, was so popular that it was selected to open the new opera house in Covent Garden six years later. Along with works such as *Le Prophète* and *L'Africaine*, Meyebeer established the model for grand opera: five-act works with ballet and recitatives accompanied by large casts, massive choruses, rich costumes, elaborate décor and even pyrotechnics. For the first time since the days of the Sun King, opera in Europe was taking its cue once again from France.

OPERETTA

Operetta, or 'little opera', also known in Austria as *Volksoper* ('people's opera') was a form of lyric theatre which attracted a huge following while *grand opéra* was conquering Europe from its base in Paris. Plundering popular waltz tunes, marches and gallops for works like Johan Strauss' *Die Fledermaus* and *Der Zigeunerbaron (The Gypsy Baron)*, it was known for its bubbly sound and comical form, and developed an international audience. Surviving well into the 20th century with works like Franz Lehár's *The Merry Widow* – still in the repertory of most opera houses – and inspiring the Victorian 'comic operas' of Gilbert and Sullivan such as *The Mikado* and *The Pirates of Penzance*, it can be seen as a precursor to the modern American Broadway musical.

ITALY: FORGING ITS OWN PATH

Even in the aftermath of the Napoleonic wars, Italy rivalled Paris as the pacemaker for opera on the continent. This was a paradox because until 1861 no such country existed. Italy was a patchwork quilt of regions and city-states, some richer, some poorer. There was however no shortage of mighty opera houses – dominated by La Scala in Milan, La Fenice in Venice and the grandest of them all, San Carlo in Naples – to feed a growing appetite for opera of every kind, from comic entertainments to great historical dramas.

The two dominant composers of the early 19th century excelled in both genres. Gaetano Donizetti left a legacy of comic masterpieces such as *Don Pasquale* and *L'Elisir d'Amore*, as well as literary and historical epics such as *Lucia di Lammermoor* and *Maria Stuarda*, inspired by the novels of Sir Walter Scott and the historical dramas of Friedrich von Schiller. Vincenzo Bellini followed suit with more eclectic fare, his version of *Romeo and Juliet (I Capuleti ed i Montecchi)* and the Scott-inspired *I Puritani* premiered in the late 1830s. Together with Rossini they would also perfect the style of *bel canto* (literally 'beautiful singing'), its dazzling vocal parts characterized by rich melodies that exploited the stratospheric note spinning and dramatic skills of its singers, and excited audiences across the continent.

It was at this moment that a young radical countryman from the farmland around Parma picked up their baton and carried it for the next four decades. Compared with the likes of Rossini or Meyerbeer, Giuseppe Verdi seemed an unlikely candidate for the sovereign of Italian opera. He came from Parma farming stock with only a brief musical tradition. He was, however, ambitious, industrious, breathtakingly gifted and in the right place at the right time. Milan was crying out for new grand opera, and it was Verdi's third commission *Nabucco*, which premiered at La Scala in 1842, that set the seal on his future. Not only was it a grand biblical epic that triumphed as a work of art, it also personified the aspirations of Italy for liberation from the Habsburg yoke – its emotional depiction of the exiled Jews touching a nationalistic nerve among those longing for an independent united Italy. *Nabucco* conquered every city in Italy and was exported all over Europe and, at the age of 29, Verdi had become the nation's principal opera composer.

Verdi described the next two decades as his 'years in the galleys' when he turned out grand operas for every Italian city and region. The formula was often predictable – a historical or biblical plot with huge crowd scenes and stirring choruses. Some like *Attila* were great successes, others such as *I Masnadieri* faded from the stage. However, Verdi forged a style of grand opera that held sway in Italy for a century. What really caught his imagination were not formulaic epics but great literature and classic drama – Goethe, Schiller and, most of all, Shakespeare. His *Macbeth* was premiered five years after *Nabucco* and bore Verdi's inimitable fingerprints.

In the early 1850s, inspired by Victor Hugo and Alexandre Dumas, he wrote three dramatic masterpieces that have not left the repertoire to this day. With *Rigoletto*, *La Traviata* and *Il Trovatore*, Verdi transformed Italian grand opera from a popular entertainment into an art form to equal the most ambitious theatre of the age. He was now not only a supreme artist but a national hero. His commissions came from the world over – Saint Petersburg for *La Forza del Destino (The Force of Destiny)*, Cairo for *Aïda* and Paris for *Don Carlos*. Even in his seventies, he was tempted back to compose his two great final Shakespeare operas *Otello* and *Falstaff*. When he died just after the turn of the 20th century, tens of thousands lined the streets of Milan. Giuseppe Verdi and Italian opera had become synonymous.

GRAND OPERA'S FINAL FLOURISH

Towards the end of the 19th century, operatic taste would begin to revert to the sentimental melodramas that dominated the early years of grand opera. Here the French staged a come-back, with Charles Gounod's *Faust*, Camille Saint-Saëns' *Samson et Dalila*, Ambroise Thomas' *Mignon* and his rather eccentric take on Shakespeare's *Hamlet* in prime position.

Dwarfing all these composers in talent if not popularity was Hector Berlioz, whose relationship with French opera houses was a rather tragi-comic one – his massive masterpiece *Les Troyans (The Trojans)* was only staged in his lifetime as a broken torso, while his most frequently performed music drama today is *Le Damnation de Faust*, which he never intended to be staged. Yet in spite of this final reinvigoration of the style, within a few decades grand opera had begun to lose its popularity and by 1900 these works had largely vanished from the stage.

AÏDA
GIUSEPPE VERDI

Celebrated as opera's equivalent of a Hollywood blockbuster, *Aïda* is an Italian spectacular with Egyptian roots. In 1869 Verdi was asked by the governor of Egypt to create an 'Egyptian' work for the inauguration of a new opera house in Cairo that was to be built as part of the celebrations surrounding the completion of the Suez Canal in 1870. A combination of missed deadlines, difficulties in casting and delays in transporting the scenery from Paris – a result of the siege of the city that took place during the Franco-Prussian War – led to *Aida* missing the slot (which was filled in the end by one of Verdi's existing works, *Rigoletto*). Finally premiered on Christmas Eve 1871, *Aida* was an immediate success, and within ten years had been performed in over 100 opera houses around the world.

Set in an undefined period in Ancient Egypt and taking a storyline from the archeologist Auguste Mariette as a starting point, *Aïda* tells the tale of a love at the mercy of public conflicts. Aïda, an Ethiopian princess, is captured and brought into slavery in Egypt – an act that forces the military commander Radames to choose between his love for her and his loyalty to his Pharaoh.

- Four acts
- First performed 1870
- Libretto by Antonio Ghislanzoni

While grounded in the conventions of French grand opera and eighteenth century *opera seria* (*see* page 53), with rousing set pieces such as its famous Triumph Scene, *Aïda* is noteable for its many large-scale duets which serve to narrow the action to a personal level – at times giving the work an almost chamber opera feel. The most memorable of these is the final act's claustrophobic aria *'O Terra Addio; Addio Valle di Pianti'* between Aïda and Radames, its short phrases brilliantly mirroring the shortness of breath that the doomed lovers experience trapped within their dark tomb.

Aïda's remarkable originality of orchestration, along with its use of harmony and instrumentation to conjure a vivid sense of place, have helped cement its place as a firm favourite in the operatic canon. Hugely dramatic and musically exciting, it is often presented on vast arenas or open-air stages in extraordinary settings, such as in front of the 3,000-year-old Temple of Amenhotep III beside the Nile in Luxor.

NATIONAL DREAMS

Italy was not the only European nation in the mid-19th century searching for its identity and finding it in opera. Opera houses sprang up in Zagreb, Lvov, Kluj and countless other smaller cities, and when Austria and Hungary united in 1867, Budapest almost equalled Vienna as an operatic centre. Responding to centuries of rule by the German-speaking Habsburgs, Bedřich Smetana, Antonín Dvořák and Zdeněk Fibich forged a Czech national style, giving pride of place to the Czech language, history and folklore which came into its own at the turn of the 20th century when the Czech lands were struggling for independence with works such as *Prodaná Nevesta (The Bartered Bride)*, *Rusalka* and *Šárka*. However, one massive nation created an operatic tradition that set it apart from all others in Eastern Europe. If grand opera was born in Paris and reached its maturity in Milan and Naples, its epic climax was almost certainly in imperial Saint Petersburg.

RUSSIA: A NEW VOICE EMERGES

Tsarist Russia was a latecomer to opera. Until the 1830s the imperial court performed mostly imported Italian work. However, by the middle of the century a great wave of nationalism swept through Saint Petersburg and Moscow, creating a unique Russian operatic style. At the centre of this revolution were Nikolai Rimsky-Korsakov, Modest Mussorgsky and Alexander Borodin, who bequeathed a unique core repertory in the

Russian language. They unearthed a rich treasury of Russian folk tales and melodies and developed a musical language that followed the rhythms of Russian vernacular speech. This gave a unique colour to their works, particularly those of Mussorgsky. Although *Boris Godunov* was his only opera completed in full score, his unfinished epic *Khovanshchina* – completed by Rimsky-Korsakov and Alexander Glazunov and staged in 1890 – and his substantial catalogue of songs still influenced Slavic opera from Prague to Moscow.

Mussorgsky's younger contemporary Rimsky-Korsakov was a more diligent worker and donated more major operas to the repertoire than any other 19th century Russian composer. He remained the most loyal follower of the Russian style but one further composer took it to unprecedented heights. Pyotr Ilyich Tchaikovsky composed what may be Russian opera's most perfect creation in his setting of Pushkin's *Eugene Onegin*, only challenged by his other great Pushkin opera – the sinister *The Queen of Spades*.

GERMANY: THE RISE OF ROMANTICISM

Meanwhile, what of Germany? More German was spoken in continental Europe than Italian, French or any Slavic language. Yet in the mid-19th century, no such country as Germany existed. It was the rump of what was once Charlemagne's Holy Roman

Empire, where more than a 150 separate kingdoms, principalities and duchies co-existed cheek by jowl. The fulcrum of German poetry, drama and philosophy was in Saxony, the home of Goethe and Schiller. However, as far as opera was concerned, in the fragmented German lands most composers and performers were poorly supported and miserably paid, and until Germany was unified by Bismarck in 1871, musical and dramatic standards varied from adequate to execrable.

The Romantic movement of the 1820s bred a particular German style, rooted in folk tales and dark legends. The prime mover here was Carl Maria von Weber whose sinister drama *Der Freischütz*, with its creepy villain and magic bullets, triggered a huge upsurge of operas based on native sources such as Heinrich Marschner's *Hans Heiling*, and influenced a whole generation of Romantic composers. Overshadowing them all, though, was one radical and fiercely ambitious young Saxon. Almost untrained and born into a not very distinguished theatrical family, Richard Wagner began his career aping popular composers like Donizetti. However, his sights were set much higher and his first significant offering *Rienzi* is a massive historical epic set in late imperial Rome which reveals itself as both a homage and a direct challenge to Meyerbeer. In the Saxon capital of Dresden it was an overnight triumph.

Wagner failed in his attempt to conquer Paris with *Rienzi* and for a decade he had to content himself with local theatres in Prussia and Saxony. Even Berlin resisted but *Rienzi*'s

YEVGENY ONEGIN (EUGENE ONEGIN)
PYOTR TCHAIKOVSKY

Eugene Onegin is considered to be Russia's most popular opera. Inspired by one of Pushkin's most beloved novels in verse, it retains much of the original's poetry, if not its satirical nature. A surprisingly intimate opera, it is also a tragic love story, concerning a selfish hero who lives to regret both his callous rejection of a young woman's love and a careless incitement of a fatal duel with his friend.

While *Onegin* evokes bourgeois country life under the Tsars, its music is decidedly urbane, lacking the spectacle and folk colour preferred by other Russian composers of Tchaikovsky's era. The score moves from gentle rustic simplicity to melodramatic intensity, but its emotional centre comes early on in Act I, when Tatyana spends the night writing her fateful love letter to her beloved Onegin. Here, over a 15-minute span, the music vividly captures all the girl's anxieties, hesitations and longing. Onegin's callous response to Tatyana's love establishes the episodic

- Three acts
- First performed 1877
- Libretto by Pyotr Tchaikovsky and Konstantin Shilovsky

opera's dark tone, while other highlights of the score include the parlour duet sung off-stage by Tatyana and her sister the mezzo-soprano Olga at the beginning of the opera, Lensky's lament to lost love ('*Kuda, kuda, kuda vi udalilis*') sung just before his duel with Onegin, along with the final-scene confrontation between Onegin and Tatyana.

In a case of life imitating art, Tchaikovsky had already begun work on Tatyana's letter scene when he received an unsolicited letter declaring undying love from a former student of his, Antonina Miliukova. Thoroughly rattled by the coincidence and unwilling to play Onegin to Antonina's Tatyana, he accepted her marriage proposal, in spite of his homosexuality. The disastrous marriage was to last three months and drove Tchaikovsky to attempt suicide, yet remarkably it was during this turbulent period that the composer was to complete *Eugene Onegin*.

successors *Der fliegende Holländer (The Flying Dutchman)* and *Tannhäuser* were more fortunate, and by the late 1840s Wagner was the most highly regarded German opera composer. However, his talent for generating huge debts forced him to leave Dresden pursued by his creditors. He was also caught up in the revolutions that exploded all over Europe in 1848, adding the role of political refugee to that of rootless transient. Fortunately, the great pianist Franz Liszt, who had been appointed Music Director in Weimar, gave him refuge and the means to complete and premiere his latest mythical music drama *Lohengrin*. Most importantly, Liszt's patronage allowed him to put on paper the first notes of his epic tetralogy of operas, *Der Ring des Nibelungen (The Nibelung's Ring)*. In addition to the 14-hour *Ring Cycle*, he also completed the greatest German operatic comedy *Die Meistersinger von Nürnberg (The Mastersingers of Nürnburg)* and the 19th century's most influential Romantic score, *Tristan und Isolde*.

While *Tristan* and *Mastersingers* were triumphantly premiered in Munich, Wagner completed the Ring and at last found the saviour who would ensure the future of his art. King Ludwig of Bavaria provided the funds to build his hero the state-of-the-art theatre the *Ring Cycle* required in Bayreuth and in 1876 he brought the cycle to a hungry international audience, followed by his final masterpiece *Parsifal*. Wagnerism was now more than an obsession – it was a religion – and would continue to be so long after the composer's death in 1883.

WAGNER'S DISCIPLES

Until World War I, opera in three continents was dominated by Wagner's followers. Among them were Engelbert Humperdinck – whose *Hänsel und Gretel* became known as a 'Mastersingers for the nursery' – Franz Schreker and Alexander von Zemlinsky. Most influential of all, though, was Richard Strauss, whose expressionist masterpieces *Salome* and *Elektra* swept through the opera houses of Europe and America, before Strauss was to turn his back on his radical self with later works including the romantic *Der Rosenkavalier*, fantasy epic *Die Frau ohne Schatten* and domestic comedies, *Intermezzo* and *Capriccio*, all still repertory stalwarts.

Meanwhile in France, Saint-Saëns, Jules Massenet, Édouard Lalo and Paul Dukas were also inebriated with Wagner, a fact evident in works such as *Samson et Dalila*, *Hérodiade*, *Le Roi d'Ys* and *Ariane et Barbe-bleue*. Even Claude Debussy's only completed opera, the symbolist *Pelléas et Mélisande*, is marinated in the score of *Parsifal*.

TRISTAN UND ISOLDE
RICHARD WAGNER

A milestone in the history of music, *Tristan und Isolde* is the ultimate glorification of a romantic love so great that it cannot be contained by the physical world. Based on the 13th century tale of Gottfried von Strassburg, it also has its roots in the philosophy of the German Arthur Schopenhaeur, as well as in the composer's forbidden love for Mathilde, the wife of his patron Otto von Wesendonck, with whom he was conducting a passionate affair.

In the score of Tristan, Wagner dissolves musical rules that had prevailed for over 150 years, opening Western music up to a new series of possibilities. From the haunting initial phrase of the prelude, the music is trapped in a constant state of tension, as if to describe the couple's desperate yearnings, and proceeds throughout to test the absolute limits of tonality with embedded harmonies so dense that it is often impossible to identify the key. As such the opera can be seen as a crucial step towards today's

- Three acts
- First performed 1856
- Libretto by Richard Wagner

atonal modern operas and was a source of inspiration for many of Europe's leading classical composers.

Tristan und Isolde's title roles are among the most physically taxing in the entire repertoire and were unlike anything heard at the time. Act I belongs to Isolde, whose furious opening aria *('Erwache mir wieder, kühne Gewalt')* can leave many singers without any voice for the warmer, more lyrical music of the second and third acts. Tristan and Isolde's half-hour duet, in which the lovers move ever closer together, forms the heart of Act II, while the final act is dominated by Tristan's ravings *('O diese Sonne')* as he waits for Isolde's arrival. The opera ends with Isolde's death in which, with all passion spent, the music is finally given the resolution that it has craved from the very beginning – the couple's love achieving perfection only in the eternity of the afterlife.

FROM WORLD WAR I
TO THE PRESENT DAY

By the end of World War I all the great world centres had their own opera theatres and styles of opera. There were now grand houses as far afield as Buenos Aires, Rio and, most of all, in the burgeoning USA, where opera (particularly Italian) was appropriated by the mega-rich magnates as a passport to high society. Meanwhile in Austria and Germany, despite the ravages of war, Alban Berg and Arnold Schoenberg both produced modern masterpieces such as Berg's *Wozzeck*, arguably the most influential music drama since Strauss's *Elektra* and *Salome*.

THE INTER- AND POST-WAR YEARS

With the Treaty of Versailles, the creation of a dozen new European nations inspired a fascinating range of diverse national styles. In Czechoslovakia, Leoš Janáček brought a new realism to music theatre with operas such as *Káťa Kabanová*, *Věc Makropulos (The Makropoulos Case)* and *Příhody lišky Bystroušky (The Cunning Little Vixen)*. In Hungary, Béla Bartók created one of opera's most powerful psychodramas in *Bluebeard's Castle*, while in the years immediately after the Russian revolution, Dmitri Shostakovich and Sergei Prokofiev added to the Russian legacy before the latter set out to find his fortune in France and America. Only one country continued much as before, undisturbed by the cataclysm in the rest of Europe. Italy remained the world's principal factory for producing lyric theatre. A new, more realistic style known as *verismo* replaced the Shakespearean rhetoric of Verdi. It had many followers but one composer dominated the repertory at the turn of the 20th century and continues to do so to this day. Giacomo Puccini made his mark early with *Manon Lescaut* and followed it with a string of popular masterpieces. *La Bohème*, *Tosca*, *Madama Butterfly* and *Turandot* proved the most reliable additions to the canon since *La Traviata* and *Rigoletto*, helped by their instant success in the USA.

The revival of opera in post-war Europe was short-lived. The collapse of the German economy and the rise of Nazism drove much of Germany's finest talent abroad. With the outbreak of World War II, the development of opera was put on hold for a second time and by the time Europe was rebuilding in the late 1940s, contemporary opera had become detached from its natural audience. Such a development wasn't helped by Stalinism, which crushed much of the most vivid operatic creation in the Soviet Union (although Prokofiev did manage to complete his masterpiece *War and Peace* in Russia despite interference from the cultural commissars).

The nations of the Warsaw Pact fared even worse, and from 1945 to 1989 only West Germany, the English-speaking world and the USA continued to deliver new work to the stage. Contemporary opera began to drift towards the margins of cultural life – a development aided in part by the advent of the gramophone, radio and television, which made almost half a

WAR AND OPERA

War has had a serious impact on the opera houses of Europe. Inevitably, German opera houses suffered most during World War II, with those of Cologne, Hamburg, Dresden and Stuttgart among dozens destroyed. The elegant Staatsoper Unter den Linden in Berlin was comprehensively trashed by the RAF but was swiftly rebuilt and now boasts an intimacy that belies its 1,400 seats, as well as a reputation for the highest musical and theatrical standards in Europe. In England too, war disrupted opera, with the Royal Opera House at Covent Garden converted for use as a dance hall, and Sadler's Wells Theatre as a shelter for homeless Londoners.

MADAMA BUTTERFLY
GIACOMO PUCCINI

In turns both hauntingly lyrical and deeply moving, *Madama Butterfly* tells the tale of a geisha bride who commits hara-kiri when abandoned by her American husband. A tragedy laced with cruelty, as with all of Puccini's works it is loved for its beauty and passion and is now firmly established as one of the most admired and influential operas of the early 20th century. The premiere, however, was a disaster, seeing Puccini accused of plagiarism of himself and others, with the composer making substantial alterations to the score before revealing a revised version (with Butterfly's husband Pinkerton's character softened) to great acclaim.

One of the great soprano roles in the Italian repertory, Butterfly requires enormous stamina – the character is rarely off stage – as well as a difficult combination of determination, fragility and charm. The opposite of the weak, delicate heroine so often seen in Puccini's works, through the opera Butterfly evolves from a state of child-like innocence to a calm acceptance of her fate, while the

- Three acts
- First performed 1904
- Libretto by Giuseppe Giacosa
  and Luigi Illica after David Belasco's
  1900 play *Madame Butterfly*

purity of her love is contrasted with Pinkerton's predatory cynicism. The role is well known for its vocal challenges, with the beaming, brilliant high notes of Butterfly's opening aria, in which she sings of her happiness at her upcoming wedding, in particular giving the singer no easy way of warming up into her performance.

Reflecting the West's new interest in Japan during this period, Puccini studied Japanese folk songs and manners in a bid for authenticity, but while he incorporates some half dozen Japanese motifs and melodies, the music remains distinctly Italian. Musical highlights include the sumptuous love duet that closes Act I (the longest and most elaborate of any Puccini opera), the orchestral outburst as Butterfly reveals the existence of her son Trouble to the American consul Sharpless, and Butterfly's 'flower' duet with her maid Suzuki, which gives way to the humming chorus of her fellow geishas and an impassioned orchestral intermezzo that accompanies her heartbreaking vigil.

millennium of operatic history available to a general audience in performances by the 20th Century's greatest interpreters (*see* pages 102–7). For the first time, it became possible to live in a permanent operatic past.

TO THE TWENTY-FIRST CENTURY, AND BEYOND

Can opera sustain a dialogue with its audiences in the same way that it did over the centuries from Monteverdi to Strauss without hiding behind the curtains of the past? This has been the most important question facing live contemporary opera since World War II. The composer who posed it most urgently was Benjamin Britten, who touched a vein with *Peter Grimes*, *Billy Budd* and *The Turn of the Screw*, all written in an idiom which seemed to combine a fairly accessible modern musical language with a narrative comfortable for audiences schooled in contemporary theatre and cinema.

A host of European opera composers have since searched for a style to match the adventurousness of post-war straight theatre. English composer Michael Tippett fitfully succeeded in finding a way of fusing a musical language that reached out to audiences with a radical dramatic style, in such works as *King Priam* and *The Knot Garden*, followed by younger British composers like Peter Maxwell Davies, Harrison Birtwistle and

Alexander Goehr, who pushed the boat out still further. In Germany, Hans Werner Henze and his younger contemporary Wolfgang Rihm sometimes managed to attract audiences to a harsher, more modern form of lyric drama. Henze's less aggressive *Boulevard Solitude* and *Elegy for Young Lovers* are still regularly performed throughout Europe, as is the remarkable surreal fantasy *Le Grand Macabre* by György Ligeti. Olivier Messiaen's huge *St Francis of Assisi* also succeeded in developing a following, although it is closer to oratorio than opera.

In America, composers flirted with Broadway drama and adapted movie screenplays to search for a way forwards, but only John Adams and Philip Glass succeeded in finding an idiom in which they felt comfortable. Adams started as a minimalist using very basic and simple materials, but soon developed a more eclectic, though still accessible, style. Glass anchored firmly in the waters of simplistic minimalism and turned out a host of successful works in every genre. His early operas *Einstein on the Beach, Akhnaten* and *Satyagraha* still command a broad popular following while John Adams's *Nixon in China, The Death of Klinghoffer* and *Doctor Atomic* have the additional advantage of video recordings still in the catalogue. Sadly, none of these has yet achieved the reach of even the most experimental of Sondheim's musicals.

At the start of the 21st century opera finds itself at a crossroads. The fall of the Berlin Wall and the rise of the internet have ushered in a new, connected era of operatic innovation as never before. In Britain, composers such as Mark-Anthony Turnage and Judith Weir are following in the footsteps of Britten and exploring new dramatic and musical territory. In Germany Detlev Glanert is demonstrating his ability to write music that is both dramatically effective and immediate through stage works such as *Caligula* and *Joseph Süss*. Globally opera composers like the Hungarian Peter Eotvos and Finnish Kaija Saariaho have reimagined the form in their own terms, while numerous productions have blurred the use of new technologies, including the incorporation of film, real-time video and digital electronics into the work. Over the past 400 or so years opera has travelled further than anyone would have thought possible. But is anyone still willing to listen?

THE RISE OF THE MUSICAL

Since 1945, only one form of lyric theatre has succeeded in maintaining a mass following – the musical. Like 19th century operetta, from which it derived, it manages to combine lyric appeal and drama to match the opera house along with large-scale spectacle. Between the wars, Harold Arlen, Jerome Kern and Cole Porter ruled the musical roost, immediately joined afterwards by Rodgers and Hammerstein, Kurt Weill and Leonard Bernstein. Today, Stephen Sondheim and Andrew Lloyd Webber occupy the peaks and troughs of Broadway and West End musical theatre. The crucial question here is whether the musical will inherit the role of opera in the 21st century or whether popular and minority paths will continue to diverge. The jury is still out.

DIALOGUES DES CARMÉLITES (DIALOGUES OF THE CARMELITES)
FRANCIS POULENC

One of the most successful of post-war operas, *Dialogues des Carmélites* is in turns startlingly dramatic, profoundly moving and rich in psychological complexities. Based broadly on historical fact, the opera tells the story of the martyrs of Compiègne – a group of Carmelite nuns who were guillotined in Paris for refusing to renounce their vocation during the final days of the French revolution's reign of terror in 1794. The libretto is adapted from a play by the novelist George Bernanos, itself based on a German novel drawn from Mother Marie's memoirs of the episode.

To capture the intimacy of dialogue, Poulenc resists the luxurious harmonic textures adopted by composers such as Wagner, and popular at the time in favour of a lean, focused sound. Vocally, the opera contains no formal arias – the dialogues themselves are largely set in carefully placed, precise recitative, with a melodic line that closely follows the text. The music's searing verbal clarity

- Three acts
- First performed 1957
- Libretto by Francis Poulenc

owes more to Stravinsky than the works of the dominant French opera composer of the 20th century Jules Massenet, with the nuns' calm chants and rituals offset against an atmosphere of threatening anxiety in dramatic fashion. A rarity in opera, here women's voices dominate (the male roles scarcely figure) and the five central characters are all carefully contrasted in vocal colour and type, from Blanche's lyric soprano to the Old Prioress' contralto.

Driven by its central themes of death and love, the opera is also rich in the erotic element of Catholic mysticism, although its attitude to martyrdom is unsentimental. The overwhelmingly powerful finale, one of the opera's few ensembles, is unforgettable; the nuns singing the lyrical hymn *'Salve Regina'* as they walk to the scaffold, their voices dropping out one by one as the distinct slashing sound of the guillotine's falling blade is repeatedly heard.

5

VIVA LA DIVA: THE STARS ON STAGE

Since the very beginning opera has been dominated by larger-than-life figures on stage. From the prima donnas of Handel's time, like Francesca Cuzzoni, to the stars of the Gilded Age such as Luisa Tetrazzini and Amelita Galli-Curci, these exceptional singers have come to personify all of opera's passion and drama, and opera fans have always responded to them with excitement and adulation. Able to command the highest fees and lay down the conditions for rehearsal, performance and even the afterlife of a new work or production, these stars – almost always sopranos (literally 'divas' or goddesses in Italian) – have played a central role in perpetuating the mysterious appeal of opera, through a combination of vocal talent and powerful, often volatile personality.

THE EARLY DIVAS

The entire diva saga can be traced back to opera's castratos, whose voices evolved out of sacred choir music and whose techniques were passed down to future vocalists through the Italian tradition of *bel canto* singing. With females in the Papal Roman states forbidden to sing in church or in public over the first 200 years of opera, castratos were highly prized, and when opera appeared in the 17th century, they readily sang both male and female roles. The most popular among them, such as Carlo Broschi, who performed under the name of Farinelli, earned cult followings in opera houses and courts throughout Europe. Opera's first 'stars', these castratos also established the rules with regard to outlandish behaviour for the divas who followed – another 18th century soprano Luigi Marchesi, for example, had such a following that opera houses would allow him to enter the stage riding a horse and singing whatever aria he desired, even if it was not in the opera he was performing.

Where women were allowed to appear on stage in the 17th and 18th centuries, prima donnas were cherished. Venice anointed Anna Renzi, the first female singer to fill opera houses; her roles include Ottavia in Monteverdi's *L'Incoronazione di Poppea*. By Handel's era, the Italians Faustina Bordoni and Francesca Cuzzoni were known throughout Europe as much for their combustible tempers as for vocal fireworks, while by the end of the 18th century Caterina Gabrielli was also internationally famous not just for her operatic performances, but having, like her castrato compatriot Caffarelli, served a brief prison sentence for outrageous conduct while performing.

The 19th century saw the gradual ushering out of the castrato but also welcomed new voice types and divas to go with them. Roles scored by Rossini produced mezzo-soprano divas such as the legendary Maria Malibran, while in the 1830s soprano Giuditta Pasta astonished La Scala with her Bellini roles. Later, the arrival of Verdi ushered in a Golden Age for the diva, with any pretender to the title needing to leave her mark on the role of Violetta in his *La Traviata*, or the title role of *Aïda*.

STARS OF THE 20TH CENTURY

While there are countless contemporary accounts of the vocal virtuosi of the past, sadly we have to rely on the descriptive skills of writers to conjure up the hypnotic power of the prima donnas of Handel and Verdi's time. It was not until the very beginning of the 20th century that recording began to capture blurred versions of great vocalism and only after World War I that there was a sound archive to chronicle the mega-divas who dominated the opera houses of the 1920s and 30s.

Gaining still greater notoriety as recording artists, the majority of these early-recorded superstars favoured Italian opera – as the most spectacular vocal displays in Verdi and Donizetti are written for high voices, this is scarcely surprising. The legacy includes Galli-Curci, Tetrazzini, Geraldine Farrar, Licia Albanese and, most of all, Dame Nellie Melba, whose international career did a huge amount to spread the cult of the diva around the globe. As sound quality improved, orchestras emerged from the aural shadows and great Wagnerian and Strauss sopranos like Lotte Lehmann, Astrid Varnay and Frida Leider joined their ranks.

At the same time, a parallel cult of the tenor developed. It originated with the pioneer producer Fred Gaisberg, who demonstrated his new invention by featuring the voice of Enrico Caruso. That wealthy and litigious superstar was soon joined by Beniamino Gigli, Carlo Bergonzi and Jussi Björling,

VOICES AND FASHION

Popular taste has usually preferred high voices. Just as castratos were flavour of the month in Handel's time, so sopranos and tenors are in ours. However, there are at least six voice types or registers, depending on the nature of the vocal instrument that produces them. Simplified, they are as follows: high lyric soprano, more powerful dramatic soprano, lower mezzo-soprano, high tenor, dramatic tenor, baritone and bass.

Of course, there are exceptions. French opera is often set much lower in the voice than Italian or Russian. A French soprano sounds more like the human speaking voice. That is why Carmen is normally sung by a mezzo-soprano, who is more likely to be celebrated for her chest voice (the lowest of the vocal registers) than her top notes. Lower voices have often been particularly popular in the Slavic world – the hero of *Onegin* is a baritone and many of the epic Russian operas feature basses in the lead role. This is just as well or 50 per cent of singers would be out of a job!

setting a pattern for tenors for generations to come. Each singer had a characteristic sound: Gigli a gleaming vocal ping; Bergonzi a combination of a rich and robust tone with a deep feeling for words; Björling a soft-grained sensitivity which could nevertheless rise to great moments. Great baritones like Mariano Stabili, Ettore Bastianini and Friedrich Schorr never had the pulling power of their tenor contemporaries, but one bass who became a major international attraction with the Diaghilev company was more than their equal. Feodor Chaliapin made few operatic recordings but he matched in many ways the popularity of Caruso and Melba, with the added attraction of the exotic Russian language and low notes that few Western singers could equal.

After World War II, UK recording companies under the leadership of the English producer Walter Legge began to ensure that all the stars of La Scala, San Carlo and Rome bequeathed us a legacy of their finest work. With access to the complete catalogue of Maria Callas from the 1950s and her great rival Renata Tebaldi who recorded well into the 1970s, we can compare the vibrant, reedy but unforgettable colour of the former with the almost instrumental perfection of the latter. In the German repertory, they are more than matched by the warm and dignified Kirsten Flagstad and the brilliantly heroic Birgit Nilsson. With the coming of stereo, producer John Culshaw made it his mission to create vivid audio versions of the complete Wagner and Strauss canon. As a result, we have

WHAT MAKES A GREAT VOICE?

While the world is full of agents, producers and coaches who think they know the answer to this question, the truth is that there are as many answers as there are voices. It is worth bearing one thing in mind – great is not perfect.

To take one example, a highly regarded tenor friend of mine sings in every continent and has recorded most of the world's great art songs from Schubert to Britten, yet he has no proper training. He learns slowly and sometimes painfully. What he does have is a vocal colour that is like no-one else – a way of shading a word or note in a musical line that is unexpected and always seems right. Sometimes this might be the result of producing the sound from a particular part of the chest cavity or alternatively using what singers call 'the head voice', where the vibrations come not from the voice-box but from the few inches between the mouth and the forehead. These technical skills can be learned and are taught in conservatoires. However, no two singers – however trained – will produce a vocal line in the same way.

Nilsson, Wolfgang Windgassen, Hans Hotter and Gottlob Frick in the *Ring Cycle*, Carlo Bergonzi, Giuseppe di Stefano and Mario del Monaco in Verdi, Elisabeth Schwarzkopf in *Der Rosenkavalier*, Nilsson in *Elektra* and *Salome* and much of the early work of Plácido Domingo and Luciano Pavarotti. The late 1960s and early 1970s were a golden age for recorded sound and many of these 50-year old readings still eclipse their modern rivals.

THE MODERN ERA

In 1990 the operatic landscape was transformed by the worldwide broadcast of the *Three Tenors* concert featuring Pavarotti, Domingo and José Carreras from the baths of Caracalla (and the bidding war that accompanied it), which spawned many imitators, not all of them equal in quality. The consequences for opera on video were not always positive. It enhanced the rise of such luminaries as Jessye Norman, Angela Gheorghiu and Renée Fleming, but it also inflated many other careers that might have benefited from a slower rate of exposure, with expectations now rising every time an impressive young singer (particularly a tenor) appears on stage.

More recently, we have begun to see the phenomenon of the 'classical crossover' star, with numerous media-savvy, high-profile singers recording and performing a wide variety of repertoire and placing an equal emphasis on their acting and singing performances. Aided by recent technological developments such as online music and video streaming and cinema broadcasting of live performance, opera, and its star performers, are now straying ever further from being the sole preserve of the houses that once contained them. Yet while opera's form, the stars it produces and the vocal styles it champions may have changed over the past 400 years, one thing remains constant – its divas continue to excite audiences and fill venues far and wide, stirring the passions that continue to ensure its future.

GIULIO CESARE (JULIUS CAESAR)
GEORGE FRIDERIC HANDEL

Handel's fifth full-length opera for England's Royal Academy, *Giulio Cesare* shows Handel at the peak of his powers. Expounding themes of warfare and passionate love, heroic action and inner turmoil, it has been called the quintessential *opera seria*, and offers lyric drama on a truly epic scale. Its wide scope is also matched by its prodigious number of arias, with Cleopatra and Caesar alone allotted eight each. Today it is the most frequently performed of Handel's operas (though it is often cut to greater or lesser degrees as it can seem excessively long to modern tastes) and remains a favourite among singers of Baroque repertoire due to its strongly drawn principle roles.

The opera's action is founded on Julius Caesar's historically documented visit to Egypt in 48 BC, although the details of the plot are largely fictional and the character of Caesar seems to be much younger than his historical counterpart. Highly successful throughout Europe during Handel's lifetime, the composer

- Three acts
- First performed 1723
- Libretto by Nicola Francesco Haym, after an earlier libretto by Giacomo Francesco Bussani

revised the score several times, adding specific arias tailored to the capacity of individual singers, including the charismatic Italian castrato Senesino, who first played the title role – one of Handel's most demanding.

First revived in modern times in 1922, initially the roles originally ascribed to castratos – Cesare, Tolomeo and Nireno – were transposed to suit basses and baritones, though more recently these have been taken over by counter-tenors or mezzo-sopranos as it has been considered important to preserve Handel's own vocal pitches. Cleopatra has provided a brilliant showcase for the virtuosity of great sopranos such as Joan Sutherland, and is a character painted with particular insight and understanding, with her two arias of grief (*'Se Pietà'* and *'Piangerò la Sorte Mia'*) among Handel's finest, while mezzo-sopranos such as Sarah Connolly have made swaggering and convincing Caesars.

6

OPERA'S OFF-STAGE EGOS: THE MAKING OF THE MAESTRO AND THE RISE OF THE PRODUCER

If opera were simply a showcase for vocal display, it might have sunk under the weight of its thousands of sopranos and tenors. Thankfully the cult of the prima donna within opera grew in parallel with another equally powerful persuasion – the rise of the conductor. In the space of just 20 years these beaters of time would come to extend their authority over the proceedings on stage, before the mid-20th century was to usher in the emergence of another off-stage power – the star director – as opera audiences began to demand a coherent dramatic vision to sit alongside the music.

THE RISE OF THE CONDUCTOR

Why do we need conductors? It's a question asked even more frequently than why opera is sung. It's also one that would not have even been understood before the 19th century. Up to this point operas did not use a large enough orchestra to necessitate the participation of a conductor, nor were the musicians placed in a deeply sunk pit, so it was enough for the singers to maintain some degree of eye contact with the first violinist or the harpsichordist, who was often the composer of the piece in question.

Yet from Beethoven onwards, the size of the orchestra grew by 50% and musical scores had become so complex that a single violinist could no longer keep the ensemble together during performance, while from as early as the late 1820s, French composer Hector Berlioz – considered by many to be the creator of the modern orchestra – was writing music beyond the grasp of anyone but himself. If one adds the extra responsibility of casting and training singers (which would previously fall to the composer), only an omni-competent maestro could fit the job description. In the absence of cloning, it soon became essential that a new class of mega-maestro was born. Fortunately, in opera's two creative capitals of Milan and Vienna, the perfect candidates were available.

MAHLER, TOSCANINI AND BEYOND

Gustav Mahler (1860–1911) and Arturo Toscanini (1867–1957) were near contemporaries. Mahler was an Austro-Hungarian Jew, born in the Moravian sticks and rising by his late 30s (after converting to Catholicism) to the directorship of the Vienna court opera. Where he differed from all his predecessors was his obsession with absolute standards and total control. Not only did his rehearsals inspire terror in artists and players alike but he also exerted the same obsessive power over design, staging and repertory. Fortunately, he was blessed with impeccable and adventurous taste, introducing the great creative figures of *fin de siècle* Vienna and the wider world to the Court Opera. His tenure was the stuff of legend for a century afterwards.

Toscanini's world was quite different. Milan's Teatro alla Scala was a commercial house and Toscanini was barely twenty when his career began but it stretched from Verdi's last premiere to the entire output of Puccini and most of his contemporaries. There are countless stories of Toscanini's tantrums. He broke batons in fury during rehearsals if performers fell short of his exacting standards, and regularly reduced players and singers to tears. However, in Italy and subsequently New York, he achieved unprecedented artistic standards. Unlike Mahler, he continued to perform until the 1950s, well into the era of the long-playing record. Thus we have an even more extensive archive from him than we do from Callas or Gigli. The acoustics may be dry and harsh but the intensity and detail of his readings of Verdi's *Nabucco*, *Luisa Miller*, *Les Vêpres Siciliennes (The Sicilian Vespers)*, *Un Ballo in Maschero (A Masked Ball)*, *Aïda*, *Otello*, *Falstaff* and many others have never been matched. As for his Puccini, he conducted the world premieres of 80% of the composer's output and brought his unique authority to everything from *La Bohème* to *Turandot*. There is no equivalent archive relating to Mahler's days in Vienna 40 years earlier, but among his achievements were bringing Wagner's *Ring Cycle* to New York, restoring Mozart to the Vienna State Opera and fostering the careers of Richard Strauss and his younger contemporaries.

Since World War II, there have been countless bids to equal the status and authority of Toscanini and Mahler. The first generation of Mahler's successors included his pupils Bruno Walter and Otto Klemperer, Clemens Krauss and Erich Kleiber, followed by the most influential of all German conductors, Wilhelm Furtwängler, whose conductorship spanned the

COLLIDING ARTISTIC WORLDS

As a crossroads of the arts, opera has often drawn on the works of 'outsiders' to deliver new looks on stage. In the early 20th century, as Modernism swept across the globe, artists such as Pablo Picasso, Henri Matisse and Salvador Dali were recruited to design decor and costumes for new works. Modern productions featuring the works of prominent artists include Peter Sellars' *Tristan und Isolde*, which incorporated large-screen videos by American artist Bill Viola, and David Hockney's famous set design for Glyndebourne's production of *The Rake's Progress*. Fashion and opera are also natural collaborative partners, as demonstrated by Giorgio Armani's stylish deisgns for Jonathan Miller's *Cosi Fan Tutte,* while sartorial luminaries such as Elsa Schiaparelli, Zandra Rhodes, Christian Lacroix and Miuccia Prada have all created costumes for operas around the world.

1930s, 40s and 50s in Berlin. Although some of their careers were stained by involvement with the Nazi regime, they all left a rich recorded legacy, particularly Furtwängler, whose complete *Tristan und Isolde* is still the benchmark for that opera. The war interrupted their career development but Karl Böhm and most of all, Herbert von Karajan have kept the maestro myth alive well into our own time. Indeed, with his obsessively controlled videos of his own performances, Karajan created a conductor cult to match that of Toscanini in impact if not quality, while in the next generation, pride of place must go to Georg Solti, Claudio Abbado, Bernard Haitink and Carlo Maria Giulini.

SUITCASES AND BROKEN CHAIRS: THE TYRANNY OF THE PRODUCER

A few years ago I was sent a small document that was doing the rounds of the opera houses. It was entitled 'How to Opera Germanly' and it sardonically shot down all the clichés of modern opera production, containing such gems as 'Avoid entertaining the audience at all costs – if they boo, you have succeeded', 'The set must be trivial, contemporary and decrepit', and, 'All characters at all times should carry a battered suitcase representing their emotional baggage.' If you have been a regular opera-goer across Europe in the last few decades, these directorial tics will be familiar to you. If you are a newcomer, it will not surprise you to hear that, with audiences declining and prices rising, novelty and shock value are at a premium.

Yet just as with the role of the conductor, the very idea of an opera producer is a comparatively recent invention. It was only just before World War I that the craft of opera producer really developed. Throughout the 18th and 19th centuries, managements normally made use of pre-existing traditional scenery, singers brought their own costumes with them and there was nothing approaching a coherent production style. The prime mover in changing all of this was Mahler in Vienna, who married musical perfection with theatrical adventure. In the early 1920s, the writer Hugo von Hofmannsthal and the producer Max Reinhardt launched the Salzburg Festival, and with it created a hunger for operatic theatre to match their spectacular productions of the literary theatre classics. Much the same was happening in Italy and France where a generation of directors was influenced by the rise of cinema to explore a visual aesthetic to equal the daring musical styles of the late 20s and early 30s.

There was one further important reason for the rise of the opera producer. With the death of Puccini, the stream of new popular operas virtually dried up overnight. Opera managements were compelled by the economics of running large houses to revive the same 15 repertory stalwarts by Mozart, Verdi, Wagner and Puccini every three years or so, and to tempt jaded palates, they looked to directors to paint familiar works in fresh colours.

DIRECTOR'S THEATRE

Following World War II, the great canon of German opera (particularly Wagner) found itself tainted by association with the Nazi regime. To distance the work from such associations, a new aesthetic order in post-war Germany threw out romantic clichés, substituting ironic glosses and holding a mirror to its own culture – warts and all – in their stead. Hence the suitcases, broken chairs, naked light bulbs and business suits that infested the productions of the 1970s and 80s. The Germans even had a word for it – *regietheater* or 'director's theatre'.

The directors were only too happy to oblige. Indeed, history had given them a mission to breathe new life into old repertory. Patrice Chéreau was already a theatre star when he directed his famous industrialized *Ring Cycle* in Bayreuth between 1976 and 1980, while acclaimed theatre and film directors Luchino Visconti and Luc Bondy also engaged in opera with notable success. Franco Zeffirelli has successfully directed both opera and film since the 1950s, while theatre director Peter Sellars has made a name for himself for his unique contemporary settings of classical operas. In recent years, film directors such as Anthony Minghella, Roman Polanski and Baz Luhrmann have all brought the pace of cinema to the opera stage, while Richard Eyre, Terry Gilliam, Deborah Warner, Fiona Shaw, Peter Stein, Stéphane Braunschweig and Luc Bondy continue to provide theatrical influence.

WHERE TO NOW?

The standard of international opera goes in waves and cycles but there is every reason to believe that we are currently experiencing a brief Golden Age. We are well served by music directors such as Riccardo Chailly in Milan, Antonio Pappano in London and Daniel Barenboim in Berlin, all of whom have left a legacy on video of their finest repertory, while today's acting and theatrical standards compared to a few generations ago are unrecognizable. Whisper it softly but, in all but the most recalcitrant houses, the various competing egos of opera seem to be finally working together.

OTELLO
GIUSEPPE VERDI

A work of masterful theatrical grandeur and technical polish, of more than 200 operas based on the works of Shakespeare, Verdi's *Otello* is considered to be the finest. Written after a self-enforced break of over 15 years, with Verdi finally coaxed out of retirement by his publisher Giulio Ricordi and the librettist Arrigo Boito (with whom he had previously collaborated on a revision of his 1857 opera *Simon Boccanegra*), it represents a departure from the composer's earlier works and is believed by many to be his greatest opera.

Throwing the play's slow-moving first act out of the window, Boito's libretto may even be seen to be an improvement on Shakespeare's original – bringing immediate focus to the work's most fascinating character, the scheming and wicked Iago, with Verdi's piercing trumpets and trombones expertly revealing everything we need to know about his malignant state of mind. Musically, *Otello* includes one of the most demanding tenor parts in the opera repertoire – the title role requiring enormous power,

- Four acts
- First performed 1884
- Libretto by Arrigo Boito, based on the work of William Shakespeare

sensibility and the ability to handle great contrasts in style. Tender and loving in places such as the love duet with Desdemona at the end of Act I (*'Già nella note densa'*), in others such as the council with Iago at the end of Act II (*'Sì, pel ciel marmoreo giuro'*) it is brazenly ferocious – a hard act for any singer to pull off, no matter how impressive their pedigree.

Although Verdi's score still contains elements of grand opera such as the big ensemble finale to Act III, it also evokes Wagner in its deeply expressive orchestral writing as well as in its use of continuous music, which enables the drama to proceed without the usual breaks between recitative and aria. Considered by many to be very old-fashioned and isolated from trends in Italian music at the time of its composition, *Otello* firmly placed Verdi back on the operatic map. An instant success on its debut run at La Scala, the audience's enthusiasm for the work led to the composer taking no fewer than 20 curtain calls on opening night.

7

OPERA HOUSES IN HISTORY

Aside from opera's composers and great singers, the single most important influence on the history of the opera has been the development of the opera house itself. More than just theatres, their ornate interiors and imposing facades have brought new works as well as much-loved classics to generation after generation. From historic European houses via classical Greek and Roman amphitheatres to architectural modern masterpieces and auditoria in the gardens of British stately homes, each makes its own individual contribution to that special sense of occasion that makes a visit to the opera so unforgettable.

THE EUROPEAN OPERA HOUSE

In the late 17th and early 18th centuries opera houses busily multiplied, starting in Venice before fanning out first across the Italian peninsula and then across the continent in their search for new audiences. Following the two models laid down in Italy and France, they were either horseshoe-shaped with boxes round the side in the Italian style – so that patrons may have a decent view of the other members of the audience – or built on an oval footprint in the French style, which combined excellent sightlines and enfolding acoustics. Yet very few of these original structures survive to this day. Why? The answer's simple. Until last century, theatres were traditionally built of wood. While

HOUSING HISTORY

Today, only three opera houses in the world survive that bear any real resemblance to the theatres in which Mozart (let alone Monteverdi or Handel) would have worked – Drottningholm in Sweden, Český Krumlov in the Czech Republic and the Stavovke or 'Estates' opera house in Prague.

Dating back to the Baroque era and continuing to put on work, Drottningholm's cycle of Mozart operas can compete with most modern productions while Český Krumlov, with its orchestra and stage hands in 18th century dress, candle lighting and traditional theatrical technique is certainly unique. Opening in 1783, the Stavovske hosted the world premiere of *Don Giovanni* and still performs Mozart's works today. Although now a 'heritage' building, more concerned with giving tourists a taste of Habsburg architectural glory than doing justice to Mozart's masterpieces, its lovingly restored red and gold interior is always crammed with visitors.

this did wonders for their acoustics it also ensured that they lasted for an average of 30 years before burning down.

Standing head and shoulders above all other opera houses built in the Italian style is Milan's Teatro alla Scala. La Scala is the centre of Italy's traditional cultural life and the tickets for its season premiere are the most coveted in the world. Every 19th century Italian composer wanted his opera to premiere there, with none more present than Verdi, and its spectacular design is only surpassed by its almost perfect acoustic. Apart from La Scala, Barcelona's Italianate Gran Teatre del Liceu, sited on the great boulevard of the Ramblas, probably had the longest history until a fire destroyed it in 1994. Fortunately, it has been reconstructed in detail following the original designs, and is once again open to the public. Other distinguished theatres following the Italian model with oval auditoria and seating capacities of less than 1,500 include Lisbon's grand Teatro de São Carlos and its older and more spectacular Naples namesake the Teatro di San Carlo. With their generous public foyers but fairly small interiors, they retain the ideal acoustic for 19th century opera, blending clarity of sound from the stage and orchestral warmth from the pit. In prime position among the others are Venice's Teatro La Fenice, backing on to the Grand Canal and rebuilt on three separate occasions due to fire, lastly in 2004, while Le Théâtre Royal de la Monnaie in Brussels runs La Scala very close for quality of sound.

Europe's principal remaining houses follow the French model, which reached its apogee in 1875 with the opening of Paris' Palais Garnier. This is without doubt the world's most celebrated opera theatre, not least because it is the setting for Andrew Lloyd Webber's *The Phantom of the Opera*. Its breathtaking decor in both private and public spaces has attracted a host of imitators, not only in Europe but also in Latin America. However, the most surprising feature of the Garnier today is the fact that it is no longer a permanent opera house. When it was replaced by L'Opéra Bastille in 1980, there was outrage across the entire continent. The Bastille was too large, too modern, its sightlines were obscured, its acoustic was uneven, it was overpriced and lacked atmosphere. Notwithstanding the opposition of traditionalists, the Bastille soldiers on a quarter century later and hosts smaller-scale opera and special events.

Meanwhile Europe also retains some successful oddities, like the private house at Glyndebourne built by the Christie family in Sussex – the new theatre built in 1994 a triumph of polished wood and exposed brickwork – and the Monte Carlo Opera, the only theatre that must be accessed via a casino. The most triumphant oddity among European houses, however, is the Bayreuth Festspielhaus, built from scratch in the mid 1870s by King Ludwig of Bavaria as a home for Wagner's *Ring Cycle* and the festival that succeeded it. It is neither horseshoe nor oval but resembles a glorified German village hall, with hard wooden chairs that give excellent sightlines, just as well during operas of up to six hours' duration. However, its acoustic, with a covered orchestra pit rising under the stage, provides a more perfect blend for the composer's mighty orchestral textures than any other house in the world.

OPERA HOUSES AROUND THE GLOBE

It was not until the mid-19th century that nations began to build opera houses outside central Europe. Russia's two great opera theatres were designed along European lines. The Mariinsky Theatre in Saint Petersburg has the most splendid of royal boxes and, as it is a variation on the horseshoe shape, the Tsar and his guests could face the stage directly. The Bolshoi only came into its own after the revolution when Moscow became the centre of government and Saint Petersburg (as Leningrad) was somewhat sidelined, with the Mariinsky only reverting to its position as Russia's prime opera house after 1989 with the combination of the fall of the Soviet Union and the rise of Leningrad heroes Vladimir Putin and conductor Valery Gergiev.

Across the oceans, opera houses developed along very different lines. In the USA, they were the product of the late 19th century Gilded Age and then the years immediately following World War I. They aspired to scale and grandeur, and with good financial justification – however munificent their patrons they needed audiences in excess of 3,000 to cover their costs. As a result, they never really matched European houses for sound, sightlines or atmosphere. The Metropolitan opera began life in a theatre in mid-town New York with a huge seating capacity of 3,625. Its successor at the Lincoln Center was slightly larger and even more glamorous. You can hear audience members catching their breath as the many chandeliers are slowly lifted to the ceiling at the beginning of each performance. However, the sound quality has never equalled the glamour, and rumour has it that electronic enhancement has been introduced to improve the balance.

The Civic Opera House in Chicago, Dorothy Chandler Pavilion in Los Angeles and the War Memorial Opera House in San Francisco are all equal to or greater in size than the Met, yet as a nation with a population of more than 300 million, it is surprising that the USA has so few opera houses and only one of recent design, albeit the very successful and welcoming McCaw Hall in Seattle. The quality of singing and orchestral playing in the USA equals the finest Europe has to offer, but after more than a century and a half, America has yet to find a distinct approach to the presentation of opera. This may have something to do with the nature of its audiences. While each major city has a powerful identification with its symphony orchestra, opera in America still seems, by and large, to belong to a wealthy elite.

A QUESTION OF SOUND

In terms of acoustics, now that almost all opera houses have adopted Bayreuth's innovation of placing the orchestra in a sunken pit in front of the stage, the most important factor is the placement of the seating, which can be seen as sitting somewhere between two extremes: the traditional French- and Italian-style Baroque theatres on the one hand and the raked fan-shape plan first used at Bayreuth by Wagner on the other.

The Baroque theatre with stacked boxes can have excellent acoustics for some, but for those sitting behind the front row in the boxes the experience is considerably muted, while open galleries are more democratic than boxes, both acoustically and socially. 19th-century designs often relied on deep overhangs, which have their advantages and disadvantages for seeing and hearing alike. The challenge in modern opera house design is to avoid these overhangs while providing a space that reverberates the sound that comes from the orchestra pit, and enabling the singer's sound to be reflected and enhanced as much as possible.

Opera houses in Latin America are in much shorter supply but have a character all their own. The Teatro Colón in Buenos Aires seems to have the best of both worlds, with grand design dating from the beginning of the last century, a seating capacity of more than 2,500 and an almost perfect acoustic. The Teatro Amazonas in Manaus, halfway up the Amazon, is tiny by comparison but for those who can afford it, the experience of seeing opera in a late Victorian house 1,000 miles into the rainforest more than compensates for the cost and difficulty of getting there.

The most architecturally splendid of all opera theatres is the Sydney Opera House. Unfortunately, in every other respect it falls short. The pit is too small and the stage too narrow to accommodate the operas of Wagner, while the acoustic is rather shallow and the sightlines less than perfect. These days it is as much used for concerts as for opera. South East Asia and China have recently began to flirt with the idea of Western opera houses, but as they have richly developed opera traditions of their own, for the time being they still prefer orchestral concerts to staged opera.

SALOME
RICHARD STRAUSS

Salome, Strauss's third opera, established his reputation as a major operatic composer. While its sensational biblical subject matter and modernist musical style led to it being received at the time of its premiere with public and critical outrage, official condemnation and even bans in several European cities, today it stands as the composer's masterpiece and arguably the first modern opera.

Skilfully trimming the text of Oscar Wilde's play down to a single enthralling 100-minute act, Strauss's libretto is by turns illustrating and probing, combining powerful characterization and grisly fascination with obsession, cruelty, and perversion. A continuous operatic 'tone poem', the action begins with the teenage temptress Salome's entrance and ends with her execution by Herod's soldiers, punishment for her murderous obsession with the prophet Jokanaan (John the Baptist). The sultry atmosphere of Herod's court provides a wealth of opportunity for musical

- One act
- First performed 1904
- Libretto by Richard Strauss, after Oscar Wilde's play

ornamentation, and throughout Strauss' huge orchestra produces exquisitely powerful effects, moving events swiftly towards the opera's disturbing conclusion.

Crucial to advancing the opera's tightly structured plot is the notorious Dance of the Seven Veils, which Salome performs for Herod in exchange for the head of Jokanaan. The dance has often been a sticking point for those sopranos cast in the title role born without the requisite gifts to do it justice, and a number have decided against performing it themselves, enlisting the help of professional dancers to act as body doubles – as did the first Salome, Marie Wittich, at the opera's premiere in Dresden. Vocally, while the role was originally intended for sopranos with the ability to power over the opera's huge orchestral climaxes, Strauss reworked the score in 1930 to make it suitable for lighter-voiced sopranos, and it is this edition that is most commonly used today.

8

OPERA FOR EVERYONE

The post-war revival of opera in Europe was hard won. With most of its opera houses in ruins, and singers, conductors and producers scattered across the world, it required a huge injection of cash and confidence to match what was taking place in prosperous America.

Yet paradoxically, Europe had the best of the deal. While the commercially-driven opera of the USA became more and more timid in its programming and predictable in its casting, in Germany, Austria, Italy and even in some of the nations under communist domination, managements were all free to take risks. Opera on the Eastern side of the Atlantic now belonged largely to the state, and because this privileged art form was now paid for by the general public, it became axiomatic it should be for everyone. Across Western Europe it became possible to see and hear artists of the highest calibre for the same price as a cheap theatre or concert ticket. This policy of artistic access had two complementary purposes. On the one hand, culture played a major role in removing the last traces of fascism left after the allied victory. On the other, it was critical in educating the new generation who would shape and govern the modern world.

Opera in Europe today is more available than it has been at any time since its birth in Mantua half a millennium ago. At the last count, reunited Germany has no fewer than 82 opera houses, not to mention dozens more small companies without permanent homes. France has 31, Austria ten and even the Czech Republic can boast eight. The grandest houses may still have expensive top prices but a stalls ticket for the opera in Hamburg or Marseilles now costs little more than a West End musical. At the other end of the scale, it is easy to find a seat in the upper parts of the house for not much more than a ticket to the movies. Yet price is only one aspect of access that has transformed the operatic experience. The allies made it a post-war priority to establish state-supported broadcasting across the whole of Western Europe. Taking the BBC as a model, for 40 years it became the norm, and two whole generations gained their musical education from public service broadcasters. There was a similar revolution in affordable publishing. The opera audiences of the 1960s may well have been the best educated in history.

One must beware of complacency here. During a recession opera is almost always the first art form to feel the pinch. Where Britain once had eight full-time opera houses, with the Royal Opera and ENO each mounting up to 20 productions every year, at the time of writing, during the Spring season, there are only 16 operas spread across the whole of England, Scotland and Wales. Compared with the cornucopia available in Germany and the generous if less profligate provision in France, the second decade of the 21st century has delivered lean times for Britain's major opera companies. However, there are always alternative ways of stimulating the appetite, and some of the highest quality work can still be found across the country. In the 1930s, the private opera house of Glyndebourne, founded by the Christie family, set new standards in England thanks largely to exiles from Nazi Germany and Austria who provided the talent to keep it open. Today, supported by the Arts Council, it tours its productions nationwide at very reasonable prices. Similar policies are pursued by Opera North, Welsh National Opera and to some extent Scottish Opera, while every year or two, Graham Vick's visionary Birmingham Opera mounts a huge production of a major work.

In recent years, cheap air travel has wrought another huge transformation upon the operatic scene. It is now possible to fly to many of Europe's top houses, stay overnight and take in an opera production for only a fraction more in total than the cost of a stalls seat at the Royal Opera House in Covent Garden. Some of Europe's most adventurous work can be seen in relatively affordable fashion at smaller houses such as Essen in Germany, while travelling further afield, the buoyant economies of Prague, Brno, Budapest, Warsaw and Krakow support opera of international class at bargain prices.

REACHING OUT TO NEW AUDIENCES

Meanwhile, a shift of focus has led to opera houses confronting the perennial problem of attracting a young audience in a variety of intriguing ways. The education departments of large companies such as the Met, ENO and ROH now reach out to school children by making special performances available at highly subsidized rates and sharing resources online, as well as taking performances into the classroom. In an attempt to woo the next generation of opera-goers, young patrons schemes offer 20- (and often 30-) somethings the possibility of behind-the-scenes access, exclusive performances and considerably discounted tickets, as well as the opportunity to meet like-minded individuals. Programming too is playing a role in attracting this youthful audience, with cross-continental collaborations such as Nico Muhly's *Two Boys* – an opera centred around the world of chatrooms and internet role play – leading the charge.

Another intriguing development is the large number of reduced versions of the operatic canon now presented in the most unlikely of venues. *The King's Head* public house in Islington started a trend for pub opera featuring a handful of soloists with piano accompaniment that has now spread across the globe. The fashion for 'underground' opera venues has since grown to include crumbling inner-city chapels and carpark rooftops, while alternative opera festivals such as Prototype in New York and Grimebourne in East London consistently challenge the perception of opera as inaccessible and elitist by offering up-close unstuffy productions of new, traditional and forgotten works. The same is true of mainland Europe, where companies such as Berlin's Kiez Oper perform in techno clubs and disused swimming pools, with the aim of reaching out to a whole new audience.

THINKING INSIDE THE BOX

Because of the commercial risks and huge financial outlay involved in staging opera in traditional houses, only a tiny fraction of new works make it onto the programmes of traditional opera companies. In the wake of the recession, many young composers have adopted a 'do-it-yourself' approach in their attempt to move beyond traditional classical techniques of singing and playing. The resulting body of work – often small, chamber-sized pieces set in small venues – has been dubbed 'black-box opera', indicating a convergence of classical composition with the spirit of experimental theatre.

While these developments are exciting and necessary, no-one would deny that opera has always floated on a sea of lavish extravagance, and mainstream audiences continue to be drawn by its traditional spectacle and sense of event. The great challenge has always been how to make this accessible to the general public at prices they can afford.

In its cinema broadcasts, New York's Metropolitan Opera has always aspired to that, though it is only recently through its pioneering broadcasting of live video of cinematic quality to local movie theatres that it has been able to deliver the sense of ownership that comes with visiting the opera house itself. Recent changes in the ownership and exploitation of opera on film and video have also had a big impact on its availability. Once the prerogative of broadcasters and then of commercial distributors – leaving the opera houses without royalties to pay for future relays – opera companies led by the Metropolitan including Opéra de Paris, the Royal Opera House and ENO have begun to invest in domestic and cinematic distribution. For the first time in 400 years, the opera house is now the joint owner of the complete opera experience. Needless to say, this has occasionally resulted in litigation and sometimes out-and-out warfare among artists and managements. In this respect opera has changed little since Handel tried to throw a recalcitrant diva out of a window three centuries ago. However, at the beginning of a new millennium, opera is probably more democratic than it has been at any other time in its history.

PŘÍHODY LIŠKY BYSTROUŠKY (THE CUNNING LITTLE VIXEN)
LEOŠ JANÁČEK

Described by Janáček himself as a 'comic opera with a sad ending', *The Cunning Little Vixen*, also sometimes referred to in English as *Adventures of Vixen Sharp Ears*, offers up a unique understanding of the natural world. Adapted by the composer from a serialized comic, the opera is built around an adventurous little vixen who, reared by a forester as a cub, escapes and raises a family. The world the vixen Bystrouška inhabits is one in which human and animal lives are entwined, and the cyclical nature of life and death is vividly depicted.

Filled with magnificent orchestral scene painting, *The Cunning Little Vixen* is deeply evocative of the richness and variety of forest life. Its poetic music – a rather dramatic move away from the often brutally serious, conversational tone of other Janáček operas such as *Jenůfa* – is light and folk-like in style, with passages of dance and mime woven into its fabric. The countless animals

- Three acts
- First performed 1922
- Libretto by Leoš Janáček after the novel by Rudolf Těsnohlídek

depicted are all given human attributes (in the case of the vixen, the need to love) and their actions, along with those of a handful of countryfolk, help bring the forest to life in spectacular fashion. In Janáček's hands the animals in the opera seem almost more human than the humans themselves, with Bystrouška in particular a delightful role for a light soprano to demonstrate a sense of vivaciousness and wild energy. Children's voices are carefully specified for the vixen's cubs and insects, long instrumental passages set different moods, while the radiant melodies echo the rhythms of human voices and animal sounds. Finishing with the forester's final paean to nature, *'Hoji, Ale neni to Bystroušky'*, and introducing the concept of death without fuss or pathos, the opera can be seen as Janáček's own coming-to-terms with his advancing years, and is a profoundly poetic tale showing a deep understanding of life returning to simplicity,

9 WHERE NOW?

Every art form has a crisis at some time or another. When photography was invented, art critics sang the death knell of traditional painting. At the turn of the last century, people were reading the last rites over the novel. Yet fiction is still hale and healthy and prices for the visual arts have never been higher.

It would be comforting to say that opera's powers of self-transformation have protected it in the same way. There are, however, some significant differences between the art forms. On the musical front, a century ago, the common language that held sway from Monteverdi to Verdi began to break down. In Western Europe, traditional harmony and melody were stretched to such a degree that they became almost unrecognizable. Schoenberg and his disciples in Vienna all but reinvented the basic grammar of music. It is true that much the same was happening in visual art – Picasso, Braque and their followers were breaking down the representative language of painting. However, artists continued to follow the old visual conventions in parallel with radical new departures. The same was the case with fiction, where writers like James Joyce and Virginia Woolf reinvented the grammar of the novel while their contemporaries continued to write stories which would have been familiar in most ways to Balzac and Turgenev.

For some reason, opera took another path. The abrasive language pioneered by Stravinsky and Schoenberg in the concert hall with works such as *Agon* and *Erwartung*

(*Expectation*) became the default mode in the opera house as well, particularly in Germany, France and the United Kingdom. This presented a challenge. The 300-year-old operatic canon was still popular and revivable. Since the 1950s opera has divided into a mainstream of familiar repertory, with a large following, and a much smaller body of new work playing to audiences a fraction of the size.

This divide was deepened by the second difference between opera and its fellow art forms. The theatre is a social space and opera is a social event. When Broadway and West End musicals became the most popular form of lyric theatre for a night out, opera began to take a back seat. In London or Vienna or Paris today you can see perhaps a couple of operas on any one night. Round the corner, you can choose from more than a dozen musicals, all easily accessible. If you wish to take a punt on Harrison Birtwistle, Wolfgang Rihm, Thomas Adès or John Adams they require preparation, patience and concentration. After a hard day's work, it is easy to see the attraction of Sondheim or Lloyd Webber, let alone all the other musical and theatrical treats on offer.

THE ROAD AHEAD

So where does opera go now? Where does it find a constituency to match the supporters of Mozart, Wagner or Puccini? There are three or four beacons to light the road but someone – whether a public body or a private individual – must take responsibility for keeping them lit. The first is, as it always has been, the music itself. The revolution in musical language which saturated concert halls and opera houses immediately after the war has itself broken down. Instead of the constant abrasion of such composers as Pierre Boulez and Elliot Carter, there is now an eclectic choice of musical styles from the dancing, multi-coloured tapestries of Oliver Knussen with his children's operas *Where the Wild Things Are* and *Higglety Pigglety Pop!*, to the hypnotic, repetitive minimalism of Philip Glass' *Einstein on the Beach* via the eastern European creations of Krzysztof Penderecki such as *The Devils of Loudun* or the Asian-influenced work of Unsuk Chin. In short, there is now pretty much something for everyone.

Sheer musical variety coupled with dramatic verve should keep new opera alive, despite the competition from other more instantly accessible art forms – in my time at English National Opera, for example, audiences were queuing round the block to see the harsh and challenging *Soldaten* by the German composer Bernd Zimmermann, drawn in by its powerful music and vibrant theatricality. But there is a third important ingredient that will continue to push opera forward over the decades and centuries to come – virtuosity. Whole new generations of singers have grown up unafraid of difficult scores or the challenging demands they make on their vocal and theatrical skills. Where once audiences queued to hear Joan Sutherland in *Norma* they now follow the multi-talented Canadian soprano Barbara Hannigan in the latest opera by George Benjamin or Toshio Hosakawa, for example.

Of course, new operatic work is always vulnerable to box-office pressure. When times are tough and money is short, audiences will always be tempted to retreat solely into Puccini or Mozart, and some opera houses will be tempted to give it to them, afraid to risk experimentation if it might mean losing them. However, this is where the fourth factor comes into play. Instead of developing attention-seeking interpretations of familiar work, many directors are beginning to explore the languages of physical theatre – from mime and puppetry in works such as Alexander Rastakov's *A Dog's Heart* to circus and the ritual dramas of Japan and the Indian sub-continent. And striking a chord with today's impecunious arts world, one of the great attractions of these exotic stage traditions is that they developed in a world rich in ideas but poor in cash.

So while the West End and Broadway continue to pursue conspicuous consumption, opera – that infinitely adaptable art form – always has a few extra cards up its sleeve. Now, as much as it has ever been, it remains opera's challenge to keep moving forward with verve and originality. It may be living through one of its most challenging periods but if it can survive two world wars, the destruction of many of its theatres and the scattering of its artistic communities, there is reason to believe that this exotic and irrational entertainment has plenty of life left in it still.

THE DEATH OF KLINGHOFFER
JOHN ADAMS

Addressing the inflammatory issue of political terrorism, John Adams' *The Death of Klinghoffer* is a thoroughly modern and extremely controversial opera. A retelling of the 1985 hijacking of the Italian cruise ship *Achille Lauro* by a group of Palestinians in which one passenger, Leon Klinghoffer, was murdered, the story is told both in 'real time' with events unfolding on the ship and in witness accounts relayed after the fact. In it, as in his previous work *Nixon in China*, Adams moves beyond the minimalist idiom of repetition and symmetry to embrace a narrative form and successfully engage with a modern opera audience.

In style *The Death of Klinghoffer* is almost an oratorio piece, with the story developing primarily through a sequence of long, meditative choruses and arias in which events are related and then considered from different perspectives. The score is rich and complex and contains a number of electrifying choruses that step

- Prologue and two acts
- First performed 1991
- Libretto by Alice Goodman

back from the action and draw instead on timeless themes of exile and nature, such as the beautiful *'Hagar and the Angel'* in Act II. Throughout, the sinuous, undulating orchestration conjures the image of the sea lapping at the boat, while in the opera's most stunning and famous sequence an aria and ballet represent Leon Klinghoffer's body falling into the sea.

The Death of Klinghoffer's religious themes, and in particular its general refusal to make predictable condemnations of the hijackers, have enraged certain audiences ever since the opening night of Peter Sellars' austere and deliberately unemotional original production at the Met. Nevertheless, in many ways the piece can be seen as extremely forward-thinking, particularly in its understanding of the fact that terrorism – both in terms of its causes and its effects on the survivors – was a subject that the arts would need to confront.

GLOSSARY

Acoustic The properties or qualities of a room or building that determine how sound is transmitted in it.

Aria An expressive melody usually (though not always) performed by a singer, with or without orchestral accompaniment.

Atonal Music not written in any key or mode. Atonal music may be written by obscuring tonal structures or by ignoring conventional harmonies altogether.

Baritone A classical male vocal type whose range lies between bass and tenor voice types. The baritone voice type is generally divided between light baritone, lyric baritone, *Kavalierbariton*, Verdi baritone, dramatic baritone, *baryton-noble* and bass baritone.

Baroque Opera Opera composed during the Baroque era, usually regarded as 1600–1750, a key feature of which is monody – music in which a solo vocalist sings the melody while other instruments provide accompaniment.

Bass The lowest classical male vocal type. The bass voice type is generally divided between *basso cantante* (singing bass), *hoher bass* (high bass), *jugendlicher bass* (juvenile bass), *basso buffo*, *Schwerer Spielbass* (dramatic bass), lyric bass, and low bass.

Bel Canto An Italian-originated vocal style that was widespread across Europe in the 18th and early 19th centuries and noted for its flamboyance and highly articulated manner of phrasing.

Black Box Opera Small, chamber-sized operatic works staged in small, often non-traditional operatic venues.

Castrato A classical male singing voice equivalent to that of a soprano, mezzo-soprano or contralto. The voice is produced by castration of the singer before puberty or a result of an endocrinological condition and the voice develops into adulthood in a unique way. Prepubescent castration for this purpose diminished greatly in the late 18th century and was subsequently made illegal across Europe.

Chamber Opera A designation for operas written to be performed with a chamber ensemble rather than a full orchestra.

Chest Voice A term used within vocal music in relation to a part of the vocal range, resonance area or vocal timbre of a singer.

Chorus A group of persons singing in unison.

Composer A person who creates music.

Conductor The guide or director of an opera to the orchestra or singer. The conductor is responsible for unifying performers, setting the tempo and shaping the sound of the ensemble.

Contralto The lowest classical female singing voice. The contralto voice type is generally divided between coloratura contralto, lyric contralto and dramatic contralto.

Countertenor A classical male singing voice equivalent to that of the female contralto or mezzo-soprano. The countertenor voice is generally divided between sopranist (male soprano), *haute-contre* and castrato.

Da Capo An Italian music term meaning to repeat the previous part of music.

Diva A celebrated female opera singer of outstanding talent. The male form, divo, exists and is usually reserved for the most prominent leading tenors.

Dramma Giocoso A genre of opera popular in the mid-18th century, developed in the Neapolitan tradition.

Ensemble A group of people who perform instrumental or vocal music.

Grand Opera A genre of 19th-century opera generally in four or five acts, characterised by large-scale casts and orchestras, and (in their original productions) lavish and spectacular design and stage effects, normally with plots based on or around dramatic historic events. The term is particularly applied (sometimes specifically using its French language equivalent *grand opéra*) to certain productions of the Paris Opéra from 1820–1850.

Head Voice A term used within vocal music in relation to a particular part of the vocal range or a vocal resonance area.

Intermezzo A composition that fits between other musical or dramatic entities, such as the acts of an opera. In the 18th century these would take the form of comic interludes inserted between acts or scenes of an *opera seria*.

Libretto The text used, or intended for, an extended musical work such as an opera, operetta or musical.

Mezzo-soprano A classical female voice type whose range lies between soprano and contralto. The mezzo-soprano voice is generally divided between coloratura, lyric and dramatic mezzo-soprano types.

Minimalism An aesthetic marked by a non-narrative, non-representational quality which originated in New York in the 1960s. Major proponents of the style include Terry Riley, Steve Reich and Phillip Glass.

Motif A short musical idea, often recurring, that has some special importance or is characteristic of a composition.

Opera Buffa An 18th century Italian term, for an entertaining all-sung musical comedy. Arising from the Neapolitan tradition of opera it was usually a full-length work, and would include lots of caricature.

Opéra Comique A genre of French opera containing spoken dialogue and arias, associated with the Paris theatre of the same name.

Opera Seria An Italian musical term referring to the noble or 'serious' style of Italian opera that dominated Europe throughout the 18th century.

Operetta A genre of opera light in both terms of music and subject matter closely related to musical theatre.

Oratorio A large musical composition for orchestra, choir and soloists similar to an opera, although strictly a concert piece with little or no interaction between the characters.

Overture The instrumental introduction to an opera.

Prima Donna The leading female singer in an opera company – the person to whom the prime roles are given. Normally, but not necessarily, a soprano.

Prologue A separate introductory section of an opera.

Recitative A style of vocal delivery in which the singer is allowed to adopt the rhythms of ordinary speech.

Regietheater A term that refers to the modern (mainly post World War II) practice of allowing a director freedom in devising the way an opera is staged so that the composer's original directions can be changed.

Score An alternative term for sheet music.

Singspiel A German language genre of opera characterized by spoken dialogue which is alternated with ensembles, songs, ballads and arias which were often folk-like in nature.

Soprano The highest classical female voice type. The soprano voice type is generally divided between *coloratura*, *soubrette*, lyric, *spinto* and dramatic soprano.

Tenor A classical male singing voice between baritone and countertenor. The tenor voice is generally divided between *leggero* tenor, dramatic tenor, *heldentenor*, Mozart tenor, and *spieltenor*.

Verismo A post-Romantic operatic tradition associated with Italian composers such as Ruggero Leoncavallo and Giacomo Puccini.

Virtuoso A singer who possesses outstanding technical ability.

INDEX

Abbado, Claudio 116
acoustics 114, 130
Adams, John 93, 147
  Doctor Atomic 93
  Nixon in China 9, 93, 150
  The Death of Klinghoffer
  30, 93, 150–51
Ades, Thomas 147
Aïda 72, 74–5, 101, 114
Akhnaten 93
Albanese, Licia 102
Alceste 63
alternative opera festivals
  139
Anna Nicole 9
Ariane et Barbe bleue 83
arias 17, 19, 36
  da capo structure 53
Arlen, Harold 95
Armani, Giorgio 115
Arne, Thomas: *King Arthur*
  58
Attila 71
Auber, Daniel Esprit: *La
  Muette des Portici* 68
Auden, W. H. 21

Bacchae, The 9, 11
Barber of Seville, The 43
Barcelona: Gran Teatre del
  Liceu 126
Barenboim, Daniel 119
baritones 103, 104, 109
Bartered Bride, The 77
Bartók Béla: *Bluebeard's
  Castle* 87
basses 103, 109
Bastianini, Ettore 104
Bayreuth Festspielhaus
  127–8, 130
Beaumarchais, Pierre de:
  The Marriage of Figaro
  14; *see* Mozart, W. A.
Beecham, Sir Thomas 39
Beethoven, Ludwig van
  64–5
  Fidelio 43, 65
Beggar's Opera, The 26
bel canto 43, 70, 100
Belasco, David: *Madame
  Butterfly* 91

Belle Hélène, La 27
Bellini, Vincenzo 101, 149
  I Capuleti e i Montecchi 70
  L'Elisir d'Amore 43
  I Puritani 70
Benjamin, George 149
Berg, Alban 45, 87
  Wozzeck 87
Bergonzi, Carlo 102, 104,
  106
Berlin
  Kiez Oper 139
  Unter den Linden 89
Berlioz, Hector 41–2, 113
  The Damnation of Faust 73
  The Trojans 73
Bernstein, Leonard 95
Between Worlds 9
Billy Budd 92
Birmingham Opera 138
Birtwistle, Harrison 92, 147
Bizet, Georges: *Carmen* 27.
  28, 42, 46–7, 103
Björling, Jussi 102, 104
'black box opera' 140
Bluebeard's Castle 87
Bohème, La 22
Bohème, La 22–3, 37, 88, 114
Böhm, Karl 116
Boito, Arrigo 120, 121
Bondy, Luc 119
Bordoni, Faustina 31, 101
Boris Godunov 44, 78
Borodin, Alexander 44, 77–8
Boulevard Solitude 93
Boulez, Pierre 148
Braunschweig, Stéphane 119
Brecht, Bertolt and Weill,
  Kurt: *The Threepenny
  Opera* 27
Britten, Benjamin 23, 28,
  45, 60, 92
  Billy Budd 92
  Peter Grimes 92
  The Turn of the Screw
  32–3, 92
Brussels: Théâtre Royal de
  la Monnaie 126
Buenos Aires: Teatro Colón
  131
Busenello, Giovanni 55
Bussani, Giacomo Francesco
  109

Caffarelli 101
Cairo: opera house 72, 74
Caligula 94
Callas, Maria 30, 31, 37,
  47, 104
Calvé, Emma 47
Capriccio 83
Capuleti e i Montecchi, I 70
Carmen 27. 28, 42, 46–7,
  103
Carmen Jones 47
Carreras, José 106
Carter, Elliot 148
Caruso, Enrico 42, 102, 104
castratos 10, 58, 100, 103,
  109
Cavalleria Rusticana 42
Cesky Krumlov Opera
  House 125
Chailly, Riccardo 119
Chaliapin, Feodor 104
Chéreau, Patrice 119
Cherubini, Luigi 68
  Lodoïska 68
  La Vestale 68
Chicago: Civic Opera House
  129
children, operas for 40
Chin, Unsuk 148
conductors 112–14, 116
Connolly, Sarah 109
Coronation of Poppea, The
  52, 54–5, 101
Così Fan Tutte 29, 39,
  64, 115
Culshaw, John 104
Cunning Little Vixen, The
  40, 87, 142–3
Cuzzoni, Francesca 31,
  100, 101

Dalí, Salvador 115
Damnation of Faust, The 73
da Ponte, Lorenzo 14–15,
  29, 64, 66
Davies, Peter Maxwell 92
Davies, Tansy: *Between
  Worlds* 9
Death of Klinghoffer, The 30,
  93, 150–51
Debussy, Claude 45
  Pelléas et Mélisande 83
del Monaco, Mario 106

158

ACKNOWLEDGEMENT

Sadly Dennis Marks died before he was able to complete this book. The publisher is grateful to the editor, Simon Davis, for writing the additional text.